C000055869

Matthew; With thanks for your support in this our
time of need. God bless all your endeavours.

Your brother in Christ.

Barry. Holy Trinity. Crossbar.
2010

CHRIST IN SHAKESPEARE

TEN ADDRESSES ON
MORAL AND SPIRITUAL ELEMENTS
IN SOME OF THE GREATER PLAYS

BY

GEORGE H. MORRISON, M.A., D.D.

GLASGOW

SECOND IMPRESSION

LONDON
JAMES CLARKE & CO. LIMITED
9 ESSEX STREET, STRAND, W.C.2

Printed in Great Britain

TO THE OFFICE-BEARERS AND MEMBERS

OF THE

WELLINGTON LITERARY CLUB

AND TO ALL THE YOUNG MEN AND WOMEN

IN MY NATIVE CITY

WHO MADE

THE DELIVERY OF THESE ADDRESSES

A JOY TO ME

PREFACE

THE following pages embody the notes which I used for a series of addresses given in Wellington Church, Glasgow, on Sunday nights at the close of Evening Service. The very large attendance, and the keen and unfailing interest displayed, have led me to publish them, in the hope that they may prove helpful to others. Though the addresses embody my own convictions, they make no claim to originality. Students of Shakespearean Literature will be the first to recognise how deep my debt is to those masters of criticism and exposition at whose feet I have sat in discipleship since my college days. I have deliberately confined myself to a few of the greater plays which one might presume to be familiar to an audience gathered from all classes of the community.

Wellington Church,
    Glasgow.
        1928.

CONTENTS

I

ON THE REALITY OF PROVIDENCE

ONE of the deepest questions man can ask is,
Does God rule the world—that is, can we detect
in history a moral and spiritual order ? Is the
universe on the side of what is good, or is it
indifferent and heedless ? Does man, striving
for the highest, align himself with Powers higher
than himself ? Is there a purpose in the trend
of history and is it moving on to moral ends, or
is it " sound and fury signifying nothing " ?

Such questions have engaged the minds of
men from the very dawn of thought. They lie
deep in every religion. They are the ultimate
enquiry of philosophy. And it is of enormous
interest to discover what was the attitude to
questions such as these of a supreme mind like
that of Shakespeare.

Shakespeare is perfectly impartial. He has no
theology to buttress. He does not set himself
to prove anything, or to justify the ways of God
to man. Shakespeare, for all the glory of his

imagination, has the truly scientific temper in his perfect fidelity to fact.

There he and Bacon are alike in spite of their enormous differences. Both reject preconceived theories, and sit down before the fact like children. And if in Bacon's case that attitude opened the way to scientific knowledge, what did it lead to in the case of Shakespeare ? That is the question we now seek to face.

It is in the Tragedies of Shakespeare that we must look for his deepest thought on such problems. They get nearest to the heart of things. In the Comedies, speaking broadly, he moves largely on life's surfaces ; taking an infinite delight in everything which is thrown up out of the depths of ocean ; quick to hear all laughter, and to rejoice in the " play-element " in things, yet never blind to the tears which even in laughter are not far away.

In the Histories he deals with life on the side of energy and action. He handles characters practical and limited ; coping with duties not outside their powers. Men fight and plot, succeed and fail, under the heaven which is above us all, and under conditions common to humanity.

ON THE REALITY OF PROVIDENCE

In the Tragedies we have the human soul as the battleground of heaven and hell. We have men set not in a limited environment, but against a background mysterious and invisible ; and there the great questions emerge inevitably. Is there a God ordering and regulating ? Is final victory to rest with righteousness ? Is it worth while striving for the best ? Is the universe indifferent to the good ? Such questions arise in Shakespeare's tragedies, not as matters of philosophy ; but because they meet us powerfully and poignantly, in every effort of interpretation.

There are two preliminary remarks I have to make, and the first of them is this : We must not think this question can be settled by what the characters in the dramas say.

It is one mark of a great dramatist that he loses himself in the beings he creates. He does not make them speak ; it is rather as if he listened to them speaking. Dickens used to laugh heartily at the comical things Sam Weller said, as though he were hearing them for the first time.

You can get at Dante or Milton through their poems : you cannot get at Shakespeare. He creates, and then his characters go their way, speaking and acting as they will. They are not marionettes, controlled by strings which are jerked by an external hand; they are free and self-determined beings. The things they say spring from what they are. They betray nothing of what Shakespeare is. They no more reveal the viewpoint of the dramatist than my neighbour's words reveal mine. To take isolated sayings of the *dramatis personæ* and find in them the teaching of the drama, is to be false to the dramatic genius. I take an illustration from King Lear. Edmund says " This is the excellent foppery of the world, that, when we are sick in fortune we make guilty of our disasters the sun, the moon and the stars" (I, ii. 128 *et seq*). Kent says, " It is the stars, The stars above us, govern our conditions" (IV, iii, 34, 5). Gloucester says, " As flies to wanton boys, are we to the gods. They kill us for their sport " (IV, i, 37, 8). Albany says, " This shows you are above, you justicers, that these our nether crimes so speedily can venge " (IV, ii, 78-80). Edgar says " Think that the clearest gods, who make them honours of men's impossibilities, have preserved thee " (IV, vi, 73-6).

Now if we try to find an answer to our question,

ON THE REALITY OF PROVIDENCE

" Does God rule the world ? " by a combination of these utterances, the only possible synthesis is self-contradictory. If on the other hand we make a selection from these utterances, we are proceeding arbitrarily, for we are not embracing all the facts. All which teaches us that we can never reach the real outlook of the dramatist by the quotation of isolated statements.

The other remark I have to make is this, that by the very nature of dramatic art Shakespeare cannot draw upon a future world for the satisfaction and consolation of his audience.

All art entails limitation. In a deep sense art is limitation. Whether in painting or in poetry, art begins in the genius of selection. And the selected field of the dramatic art is the compass of this mortal life, from the cradle to the grave.

Virgil can travel into realms unseen, and does it with magnificent imagery. Dante can justify the ways of God with man in the continuance of existence after death. Shakespeare, true to the art which he has chosen, cannot avail himself of such resources to ease the mental pressure of the tragic.

He is at liberty to use it in so far as it motives

human conduct. He is not at liberty to use it as an appeasement or an explanation.

That does not mean that the dramatist has no personal faith in such a world. He may believe in it intensely : it may be one of his articles of faith. It means that he is supremely true to the form of art which he has chosen, and refuses to pass beyond its limits.

No tragedy can close with prophecy, nor place its ultimate issues in eternity. It must find in this present shadowed life the abiding and eternal values. Success and failure, triumph and defeat, order and chaos, heaven and hell, all these, in dramatic literature, must be here and now—the rest is silence.

The first thing to be said, in endeavouring to give an answer to our question, is that in the tragedies of Shakespeare we are conscious of powers not ourselves.

The characters are not isolated beings, nor is human society their one environment. They are urged and hindered, incited or repressed, by powers that are supernatural. The student of the plays grows deeply conscious that human action has its unseen environment, and runs away into spiritual mysteries. This effect is due to

16

many causes, and I can only indicate one or two of them.

There is the presence in the plays of supernatural visitants, or of apparitions that bespeak a realm invisible. There is the ghost of " Hamlet," the witches of " Macbeth," the apparition of Banquo at the feast. Such things, in the combined impression that they make, take the mind beyond things seen and temporal, and hint that life is more mysterious than we know.

Such appearings are not meant to be illusions, the outward symbols of our inward state. Often there is nothing in the inward state that could suggest, or account for, the intrusion. They are not psychological, they are objective. They are the dramatist's way of revealing to his audience that his characters move in a dim, mysterious universe, where there are things which philosophy has never dreamed of.

Whether he himself believed in ghosts and witches is a matter quite beside the point. He uses them dramatically, for their suggestive power. If through them he can touch his audience with an awed sense of mysterious environment, their use is dramatically justified.

Then there is the sympathy of nature with human passions and experience, so noticeable in all the tragedies, and most conspicuously in King Lear. Inward agonies are thrown against a screen where nature herself is in an agony. Storms within have answering storms without; night in the soul blackens the skies above. And this so strange and awful correspondence not only heightens poetical effect, but serves to link up suffering and action with the unseen powers that are sovereign in the heavens.

It is not by chance that a tempest-driven soul finds itself in a tempest-driven world. It is a hint of unfathomable correspondence between human life and the mighty powers without it. We feel, reading, as we are meant to feel, that the universe is not indifferent to the sins and struggles of the soul.

Then when to these things are added such words as we have cited from King Lear, not as revealing the dramatist's religion, but as expressing the consciousness of those who speak them, we feel that the soul cannot detach itself from the unseen and spiritual world, nor escape the impact of its influence.

ON THE REALITY OF PROVIDENCE

There are powers not ourselves moving in the lives of men, girding, guiding, and restraining, though men often are quite unconscious of them. All which is crystallised in the familiar words of Hamlet :

> There's a divinity that shapes our ends
> Rough-hew them how we will.

There is one feature of the tragedies that might seem to tell against this view of things. It is the determinative power of accident.

Not infrequently, in Shakespeare, tremendous consequences are made to follow from the kind of " happening " that we call accident. Juliet awakes from her unconsciousness a minute too late. Hamlet has a chance-encounter with a pirate-ship. Had Edgar arrived a moment sooner, the life of Cordelia would have been saved. Desdemona drops her handkerchief. And one might ask " If life and death depend on accidents like these, can it be held that God rules the world ? "

The rulership of heaven implies purpose (whether good or bad has yet to be considered). It is incompatible with the belief that there is any determinative power in chance. And yet Shakespeare makes mighty issues hang on things that seem entirely purposeless, and out of any relationship to will.

On the other hand one must remember that Shakespeare is no theorist. He is intensely true to fact. He sees life steadily and sees it whole. And no portrayal of life would be complete that did not admit into the picture the presence and power of what we call accident.

Such facts are here, and must be reckoned with, whatever our view of God and of the universe. Wordsworth for instance recognised them, and found a place for them within his faith. And their presence in Shakespeare (as in Wordsworth) does not reveal his thought of the unseen. It reveals his fidelity to life.

It is an easy thing to build a faith when one makes a selection of the facts. But the only faith that is of solid worth is the one that faces every fact. And that is the glory of Shakespeare (as it was the glory of our Lord) that he goes open-eyed through life, and refuses to be blind to anything.

One conclusion which to me seems certain is that this unseen power is not fate. One never feels in reading the great tragedies that everything is predetermined.

ON THE REALITY OF PROVIDENCE

The thought of fate implies that man is helpless, and his deeds necessitated. He is driven and not free. He has no hand in shaping his own destiny. He is constrained by powers external to himself, just as a motor is urged and constrained by one who uses its intricate machinery, and yet is always other than the car.

In Greek tragedy we find such fatalism; a resistless power behind the gods; a dark, inevitable necessity which uses men as pawns. But in Shakespeare, however dark the sky, however incalculable the ends of human action, men are never driven to their deeds by an external necessity like that.

If they were, then the issue of the tragedies would leave us rebellious and blaspheming. Like Job we should be tempted to curse God and die, in the deaths of Cordelia or Desdemona. But nobody leaves a tragedy of Shakespeare a prey to atheism and despair. He leaves it awed and pitiful and reverent.

Unseen powers do not determine destiny, however powerful these influences be. Man is his own destiny. The issues of life are in the heart. The only fatality Shakespeare recognises is the fatality of character, revealing itself in self-determined deeds.

Othello, for all his noble qualities, was responsible for doubting Desdemona. Macbeth was harbouring dark and guilty dreams before the witches met him on the heath. It was not the gods who inspired the delay of Hamlet, with all the woe and bloodshed which attended it. Lear was far more foolish than his fool, in his ridiculous handling of his daughters.

To Shakespeare this was an inexorable universe. There was no door of escape from consequences. No one ever saw more clearly that as a man sows, so shall he reap. And much of the power of his tragedies lies in this, that he saw with such supreme fidelity that such reaping does not only follow open sin.

It follows the harbouring of evil thoughts, as in the instance of Macbeth. It follows procrastination of obedience, as in the case of Hamlet. It follows those who let themselves be gulled, as Othello let himself be gulled. It follows selfish stupidity as with King Lear.

Whatever the powers not ourselves may be, however dim and awful and mysterious, they never damn a man or bless a man in independence of his character. All which suggest to us, as Greek tragedy never does, the God of the Old Testament and of the New.

What then can we positively learn from Shakespeare of the nature of the power not ourselves ? We shall consider that in our second lecture.

II

ON THE CONCERN OF GOD

THE question we have now to consider is this:
what is the nature of the power that rules the
world, or to put it in more abstract language,
is there a moral order ?

I have already touched on the importance of
finding an answer to that question. Shakespeare
has no theories to uphold. He is emphatically
not a theologian. He brings a mind of enormous
power to bear upon the whole range of the facts
of human life. These facts he sees with the
clearest eyes, undimmed by prejudice or
partiality; eyes that are never dazzled by
appearances, nor averted from what is horrible.

It has been said that men should be divided
into those who see and those who do not see.
Shakespeare is the lord of those who see. It is
therefore a matter of profoundest interest to
discover what human life revealed to him of the
power that lies behind all human action.

Is it a power that is friendly to the good ? Or

is it a power in sympathy with evil ? Or is it a
power morally indifferent to aspiration or vicious-
ness ? That is the question we have now in hand.

I might note in passing that in the tragedies
of Shakespeare we do not find what we call poetic
justice. If we did, of course the plays would not
be tragedies.

In novels, almost without exception, you have
a happy ending to the story. Evil is punished
and virtue is rewarded, to the entire satisfaction
of the heart. And the certainty that, before the
curtain falls, villainy is going to get its due, has
a twofold effect upon the reader.

In the first place it sustains him through the
intermediate overthrows of goodness. He knows
that all is going to come right, and knowing it,
is comforted.

But in the second place that very knowledge
prevents him from full surrender to those feelings
which the facts of life are fitted to evoke.

The average reader is irritated if the novel he
is reading does not turn out well. There is a hint
in that irritation of the heart's assurance that
heaven is on the side of what is right. There is
also a hint that what the reader sought was a

shelter from this weary world, where poetic justice is so seldom visible.

In Shakespeare you have no such shelter. If you walk with him, you have to face the blast. Tragedies do not end in wedding-bells. We do not purr at the close like Edgar's cat. Rather we feel how different life would be if we were in the place of power, and could remould things to our heart's desire.

Have you never wished that Juliet might live, or that Lear and Cordelia might at last be happy ? For a hundred years King Lear was acted so— it was altered to give a happy ending. But Shakespeare never gives you that—he refuses the fiction of poetic justice. And the refusal is the measure of his genius.

He never gives little answers to great questions. He never leaves you purring. If he did, he would be false to life, which very seldom leaves anybody purring. It may leave you victorious yet miserable ; it may leave you crucified yet crowned ; it seldom leaves anybody (as the novels do) in a smug and limited contentment.

Far better than any shallow satisfaction is it to feel the mystery of things. It is better to be awed than to be doped. The little room may be warm and bright and comfortable. But vision and exhilaration are in the storm and sunshine of the hills.

Is then God indifferent to moral issues ? Let us take that question first. And let me say quite frankly that in the tragedies there is not a little which seems to point that way.

Macbeth attains the apex of his hopes, and mild, good Duncan is murdered in the night. Iago accomplishes his villainy, and virtuous Desdemona dies. Lear, in his old age, seems to move under a regardless heaven, and is loaded with sufferings which drive him mad.

We are forced to ask the question, does God care ? Has He any interest in these various lives ? Is He heedless of what is happening on earth ? Does He feel any concern in it at all ? Or must we say, as the Jews cried at Babylon, in the bitterness and despair of exile, " My ways are hid from the Lord, and my judgment is passed over from my God " ?

One recalls the despairing cry of Carlyle, " I would believe in God if He did anything—but He does nothing." Are we not prone to feel, as we read Othello or King Lear, that " He does nothing " ? And yet I venture to say that whatever Shakespeare shows us, about the mysterious facts of life, it is not the moral indifferentism of heaven.

For in the first place outward success and failure are not the measure of the regard of heaven. The rewards and penalties of heaven are inward, and move within the region of the soul.

If Macbeth, winning his heart's desire, were left with a tranquil and expanded heart ; if in the outward triumph of his hopes he had the inward triumph of his spirit ; then it would be reasonable to hold that heaven was indifferent and regardless.

But the horror of the tragedy is this, that in accomplishing the evil he was set on, all that makes life beautiful departs from him, and he moves down into the darkness of the night.

Be sure your sin will find you out, says Scripture. It does not say your sin will be found out. It says that sooner or later it will find you out, in the deep and secret places of the soul. And the awfullest horror in " Macbeth " is not the murder of the helpless Duncan ; it is the way in which Macbeth's sin found him out.

His soul shrank and shrivelled; all that was sensitive in him turned to stone; he became the prey of agonising fears; he could not sleep—"Macbeth hath murdered sleep." Suspicion haunted him; terror was round about him; life was a living death. He lost all kinship with what was fair and lovely; he "made his bed in hell."

Remembering that, how can one believe that to Shakespeare heaven is morally indifferent? How can one say that God does nothing? Such judgments are entirely invalid unless one deliberately ignores the soul, and that is what Shakespeare never did.

To him outward success and failure are no criterion of the ways of heaven. It is not in such things that the hand of God is shown. It is in the enrichment or impoverishment of soul; in inward life or death; in the heightening or the lowering of being.

In that sphere God is not indifferent—that is the awful terror of Macbeth. In that sphere the Power not ourselves displays what it loves and what it hates. No outward triumph, no success, no attaining of what the evil heart is set on, interferes for an instant with the truth, be sure your sin will find you out.

Or again, take the fact of suffering, as we see it in King Lear. One is readily tempted, as one reads of it, to credit the indifference of heaven.

That an infirm, white-haired old man should be allowed to suffer as King Lear suffers; that the pitiless elements should break upon him, when already broken by his pitiless daughters; such experiences at once suggest the thought that God, like Gallio, cares for none of these things, and is altogether regardless of mankind.

There seems to be no hint here of a watchful and observing Providence. There is no eye to pity and no arm to save this poor, old, broken man. God, one might think, never interferes; lets things go on without a sign of interest; sits supremely regardless in the heavens.

But the instant we begin to look a little deeper, we discover that this is not all the truth. Just as sin reacts on Macbeth's soul, so does suffering on the soul of Lear. It purifies his soul; quickens his vision; deepens and extends his sympathies; drives him to his knees in prayer.

I think Lear suffered more in his prosperity than in the bitter days of his adversity. Power had blinded him; made him rash and headstrong;

made him disdainful, arrogant, contemptuous. And nothing is more beautiful in Shakespeare than the purification of the soul of Lear under " the slings and arrows of outrageous fortune."

For the first time he begins to know himself ; he sees where he has failed ; contempt passes into a sense of brotherhood ; he grows considerate and pitiful and patient. And all this springs from that very anguish which, on a superficial view, tempts us to think that heaven does not heed.

It is the same problem as met us in Macbeth, only now we view it from the other side. There by sin a soul was lost : here by suffering a soul is saved. But in both cases the interest of heaven is discovered not in outward fortune, but in the realm of the interior life.

You must dwell deep if you are to dwell with Shakespeare. You must be willing to revise your scale of values. Shakespeare felt, just as our Lord felt, the infinite value of the soul. Once grasp that, and read him in the light of it, and you begin to see how ridiculous it is to regard him as a pessimist, proclaiming the indifference of heaven.[*]

* See the treatment of the subject of Pain in Martineau, Study of Religion II; Hinton, Mystery of Pain ; A. B. Bruce, The Providential Order.

Or again take the tragic fact that evil involves those who are good. No fact is more patent in the tragedies.

If the consequences of evil could be exhausted in the evil-doer, that in itself would proclaim a moral order. But in Shakespeare, as in life, there is no such limiting of consequence—the good and evil are alike involved.

Romeo and Juliet pay the penalty of the faction of their houses. Lady Macduff and her innocent little son suffer for the evil in Macbeth. Pure and beautiful souls like Desdemona have to die because Iago is a villain. Cordelia perishes not less than Regan.

Can heaven really care, when suffering is indiscriminate like this ? When men are involved in common ruin, can there be a Power that distinguishes ? One gets relief from this desolating doubt by the thought of the solidarity of man.

If men were isolated units, all social life would be impossible. All that is fair and beautiful and helpful in social life springs from the fact of solidarity. And the embracing woe that evil brings is but the other side of that great fact on which the richness of society depends.

If we trace the hand of heaven in the family,

32

and in the ordered life of church and state; if friendship and love and parenthood and citizenship appeal to us as the good gifts of God; can we not accept, with undiminished faith, the darker consequences of that solidarity, without which life would be intolerable?

Is then God on the side of what is evil? Let us take that question next. And here we are met by a feature of the tragedies too common to be accidental. I mean that its frequent occurrence seems to indicate that it powerfully engaged the thought of Shakespeare, when brooding on the mysteries of life.

When a nurse makes things easy for the patient, that shows she is on the patient's side. It was the characteristic of Mrs. Gamp that she did not make things easy for the patient. So when heaven makes things easy for the evil-doer, and deftly opens doors of opportunity, one might be naturally tempted to infer that heaven is on his side.

Now no one can diligently read the Tragedies without noting how often that occurs. Heaven does not bar the door to evil; it often puts its finger to the latch. By coincidence, by happy chance, by favouring gales of circumstance, it seems to smile on the evil of the evil-doer.

The witches met Macbeth when he was flushed and radiant with success. Duncan announced he was going to be his guest, and so doing gave him his opportunity. Bianca appeared upon the scene at the very moment when the villain needed her. Edmund had opportunities to hand.

What do we make of all those favouring chances ? Are men being led into temptation ? Does Shakespeare imply in bitterness of soul that the world is cursed with an immoral order ? There are two things to be said on that.

The first is that such favouring circumstances do actually occur in human life. Had Shakespeare ignored them altogether, he would not have been faithful to the facts.

The second is that such favouring circumstances never make the evil ; they only occur and offer themselves when the heart is already set on what is evil.

It was not the visit of Duncan to Macbeth's castle, that awoke the thought of murder in Macbeth. It was not even the prediction of the

witches, prophesying that he would be the king.
Macbeth already was a guilty man ; murder was
in his heart ; he was dreaming evil desires of
usurped sovereignty.

It is wrong, therefore, to make God responsible
for the opportunities that favour evil, as if He
deliberately opened doorways to encourage and
invite the evil-doer. All life is full of open
doorways, some opening on heaven and some on
hell, but always it is the man himself who settles
whether or not he is going to enter in.

To the good there are avenues towards goodness
opening from the highway every day. To the
bad there are incitements towards evil in things
indifferent or even beautiful. To charge God
with being on the side of evil because such are
the conditions of our life, is to charge Him with
an act of folly in bestowing on His children moral
freedom.

Can we then hold that the dramatist's con-
viction was that the unseen Power makes for
goodness ? For him was there a moral order in
the world, spite of all its obscurity and tragedy ?
First let us consider this, that evil is the source
of all disorder.

Take Romeo and Juliet, for instance : it is not their love that leads to all the agony. It is the devilish and sinful animosity between the houses of Capulet and Montague. Love ennobles, purifies, redeems, even though it lead to sacrifice. Evil alone ruins and destroys.

It may be the evil of indecision, as with Hamlet ; or that of ambition as with Macbeth. It may be the evil of jealousy as with Othello ; or that of ingratitude, as in King Lear. But always the power that mars the world, and wrecks things, and paves the way to ruin, is the power of what is bad.

Now if my motor-car gets out of order, if something deranges and disturbs its mechanism, I know at once that the deranging factor is inimical to the conception of its maker. And if evil, everywhere and always, deranges and disturbs the world, the same conclusion reasonably follows.

If the order of the world were an immoral order, evil would assist its better functioning. But that is precisely what it never does for Shakespeare. It wrecks and ruins and destroys. Who can doubt then that even in his tragedies Shakespeare recognised a moral order, and knew that heaven was on the side of what is good ?

ON THE CONCERN OF GOD

Again there is the fact of conscience, and everything which that implies. And nowhere in our literature is the power of conscience more superbly pictured than in Shakespeare.

Think for instance of Macbeth, immediately after he has murdered Duncan. He hears the watchmen asking God to bless them, and he cannot say Amen. It is one of the profoundest touches in the drama, that Macbeth awakes to the consciousness of guilt through the discovery that he cannot say Amen.

He feels that to say it would be mockery, and he feels so because he is a murderer. Had he been saving Duncan's life, instead of taking it, the word would never have stuck fast in his throat. It is Shakespeare teaching us, through conscience, that even villainy is conscious that God is on the side of what is good.

Macbeth knew that heaven was against him, spite of the sophistications of his wife. He felt, as David felt, " Against Thee, Thee only, have I sinned." And to confess that, is to confess that God is good, and is governing the world in righteousness, though clouds and darkness are about His throne.

Lastly note how Shakespeare wins our love for what is good and beautiful and noble, and in so doing liberates the soul from the oppression and dominance of evil.

If our sympathies were with Macbeth, it would be hard to credit that the world is good. If the heart acclaimed Iago as a hero, ideals would be immoral. But nobody loves Iago or Macbeth, however profoundly we may pity them : it is Duncan and Desdemona whom we love.

Regan and Goneril achieve their ends, yet in these ends we never acquiesce. We hate them ; our soul rebels at them ; our hearts, unsatisfied, raise a continual protest. And that instinctive protest of our being against what is cruel and cowardly and beastly, is Shakespeare's assurance that goodness is the deepest thing in the world, and in man who is its crown.

There, I venture to assert, Shakespeare is a truer guide than Milton. For Milton's Satan has splendid touches in him, that wrest an unwilling admiration. But Shakespeare's Satan is altogether hateful ; he is mean and cowardly and evil : and the heart protests against him all the time.

Goodness may be vanquished, but our heart

remains upon the side of goodness. Evil may be victorious, but we loathe it even in its victories. In the dark mysteries of many-coloured life, man at his deepest sides with what is good, and so doing aligns himself with God.

If Shakespeare left us sullen and despairing, we might flee for refuge to the gods of pessimism. But that is precisely how he never leaves us, though the stage be strewn with the bodies of the good. He leaves us with the glowing certainty that the good are the real victors though they perish, and that heaven, though dark with cloud, is on their side.

III

ON THE NATURE OF MAN

IF our blessed Lord has laid us under an incalcul-
able debt by the thought He has given us of God,
He has laid us under a like debt by the thought
He has given us of man.

The two indeed are vitally related. According
to one's conception of God will be the view he
cherishes of man. If the Supreme Being be that
of Epicurus, man cannot possibly be great. On
the other hand if man be worthless, and devoid of
spiritual significance, the wisdom and love of
God suffer eclipse.

Wherever there is a lofty thought of God, there
follows a lofty thought of man. The two are
inextricably interwoven both in philosophy and
practice. We should therefore expect to find in
Christ who has revolutionised our thought of God
a revolutionary view of man.

I propose in this lecture to touch briefly on some
of the salient points in our Lord's view of man,

and then to see to what extent these are illustrated and exemplified in Shakespeare.

I begin by mentioning one point of difference which displays the pre-eminence of Jesus. There is a glowing hopefulness in the outlook of our Lord, for which in Shakespeare one seeks in vain.

One might say this is inevitable when we are moving in the realm of tragedy. If men repented and turned from their evil ways, that which forms a tragedy would vanish. But neither in the histories nor in the comedies have we any clear and definite recognition of that great fact in life we call conversion.

Christ was severe just as Shakespeare is. He proclaimed an inexorable law. He knew that sin is death, and that as a man soweth, so shall he also reap. But side by side with that, in Christ, there is a hope of rescue for the vilest, which is not recognisable in Shakespeare.

Macbeth shows no traces of repentance, even when he is told his wife is dead. Iago, to the last, has a heart hard as the nether-millstone. Regan and Goneril are never visited by any yearning to be right with God again—they pass on, hardened, to the night.

That is to say you do not find in Shakespeare what thousands of sinful men have found—a power that can redeem, and save the vilest and most hardened heart. And yet this—this unconquerable hopefulness—this grace that can redeem —is of the very genius of the gospel.

Hints of it you have in Shakespeare, in the ennobling efficacies of human love; in the assertion of the higher self under the summons of responsibility; but of the divine act of saving grace, whereby a man is born again, there is no instance in the plays.

Having acknowledged this, I go on to ask what is distinctive in our Lord's conception. And the first thing to be said is this, that our Lord centred on the individual.

We speak much to-day about humanity; but our Lord spoke little of humanity. His chosen way to influence humanity was to grapple with, and influence, the one. The common life of congregated thousands stirred Him to the depths. He was moved with infinite compassion towards them; they were as sheep without a shepherd. But He never wrought upon the scale of thousands; nor expected miracles from mass movements ; He always wrought upon the scale of one.

He gave His richest to audiences of one. He chose His disciples one by one. For one coin the woman swept the house ; for one sheep the shepherd went aseeking. The mark of Christ is that with a social aim and with His heart set on establishing a kingdom, He insisted with a passionate insistency on the place and power of the individual.

Now so is it with Shakespeare. Shakespeare is the most intense of individualists. The crowd did not even move him with compassion ; there are traces that it moved him to contempt. For him all that is beautiful in life, and everything that confuses and deranges it, roots in the depths of the individual soul.

The desolation and misery of Scotland run back to the evil in Macbeth. The times were out of joint in Denmark because a woman gave herself to incest. The bloody feud of Capulet and Montague ceased, and was replaced by amity, because Romeo and Juliet loved.

Shakespeare insists upon the one ; he is the impassioned prophet of the one ; he recognised

that social good and evil are the outflow of the
single soul. And this, the recognition of personality as the dynamic of society, recalls, and not by
accident, the teaching of our Lord.

Again it is a mark of Jesus that He recognised
the worth of man. For all his failures and his
follies man was never contemptible to Jesus.

The worst man, and the most sunken, was to
Him a potential son of God. It was not for an
elect few He lived, nor was it for an elect few He
died. And this recognition of the worth of man
is all the more remarkable, because of His perfect
knowledge of the heart.

Sometimes we say, " Had I but known, I should
never have let that man cross my threshold."
We could not read his secret, and therefore were
mistaken in our judgment. But our Lord " knew
what was in man," was never mistaken in His
judgments, and yet drew him across the threshold
of His love.

Now the singular thing is that in Shakespeare
you discover a corresponding estimate. Man to
Shakespeare is never a poor creature. He may
be hardened, cruel, wicked ; he may be set on
deeds of villainy, but nobody ever closes one of

Shakespeare's tragedies with a depressing sense of the littleness of man.

If one did, then reading them would wilt the soul. We should be prone to turn to pessimism. But Shakespeare never makes anyone a pessimist, though villainy may seem to walk triumphant. He leaves one conscious of a larger world, and of mighty forces moving in the darkness, and of man a little lower than the angels.

All man's follies and absurdities he knows ; all the evil brooding in his heart. He confronts human nature fearlessly, and is faithful to everything he finds. Yet it does not make him cynical or sceptical, as it has done with so many lesser minds. It leaves him moved, just as it leaves the reader, with the inalienable grandeur of the soul.

To that must be added that our Lord saw the worth of man, because He was (and is) " the lover of the soul."

We never see rightly till we love. When we hate anyone, vision is distorted. When we are indifferent, the eye is dim. Only when we love do we discover the hidden treasuries of personality. And Shakespeare is a far-off follower of Him who loved, and saw what no one had ever seen before.

45

CHRIST IN SHAKESPEARE

Shakespeare is not contemptuous of man, though he is perfectly aware of all his fooleries. He is not coldly critical, nor loveless, nor ready to condemn. He is filled with a profound and loving sympathy for everything that is human, and because he loves, he understands.

Think of the care he bestows on secondary characters : they are precious to him although they be not heroes. They cross the stage and live, because of their place in the creator's heart. Mercutio is just a passer-by, with no vital connection with the story, yet we all love Mercutio because Shakespeare loved him, and so made him live.*

Again when you love anybody, you want him free (where the spirit of the Lord is, there is liberty). You could never bind in chains of iron anybody who was dear to you. And just because Shakespeare loves his characters, he lets them walk away in perfect liberty, sometimes to the hazard of the plot.

* The Nurse and Mercutio are nothing in the original tale. Here they become living representatives each of a separate class. As vivid and as distinctive a life is given to the rest, down to the very servants. None resembles the others. All have their own ways, their own character, their own results.

STOPFORD BROOKE, Ten Plays, 37, 8.

ON THE NATURE OF MAN

Shylock in the interests of the plot ought to have been a monster of cupidity. We ought to hate Shylock with an utter loathing, if the dramatic effect were to be perfect. But then Shylock caught the heart of Shakespeare, and moved him to a pitying compassion, and in that poignant feeling we all share.

In his loving care for secondary characters; in the liberty he gives to his creations; in his refusal to condemn on imperfect or superficial evidence, Shakespeare betrays that strong, deep love which alone is capable of seeing that man is greater than he knows.

In this same connection I think again of Christ's estimate of values. We have to recast our scale of human values if we are ever to have the mind of Christ.

The world estimates value by possessions; it places the chief end of man in happiness; brilliant intellectual gifts are necessary if one is to stand high in the scale of values. But the one thing that really matters to our Lord is character. He did not live and die to make us happy, though happiness be found as a by-product. He did not teach the way to become brilliant, nor the secret that makes the millionaire. By His life and death He unlocked the brazen gates that debar man from being his highest self. He proclaimed the sovereignty of character.

Now Shakespeare does not proclaim things, for a poet is not consciously didactic. With perfect truthfulness he shows us men and women in the intricate relationships of life. And the singular thing is that when we walk with Shakespeare, as so many humbly try to walk with Christ, we have at once to revise our scale of values.

We learn that man is not here to be happy, though there is a great deal of happiness in life. We learn that men may fail and yet succeed ; or succeed and yet be pitiable failures. We learn that everything runs back to character and that character is fate—that what a man is, determines everything.

What shall it profit a man, said our Lord, if he gain the whole world and lose himself ? The world disbelieves in that comparison, and constantly acts upon its opposite. But Shakespeare, in grim and awful fashion, illustrates the truth of it, and as a dramatist takes his stand with the Lord Christ.

ON THE NATURE OF MAN

Macbeth gains his world—he wins the crown of Scotland—he climbs to the height of his ambition. In doing so, he loses his own soul—his nobler and better self is slain. And as we gaze on his fears, his haunting terrors, his hardening of heart, his life in death, do we not catch ourselves whispering, What shall it profit a man ?

Shakespeare is not out to teach that lesson. He is a poet and never thinks of teaching. He is out to grip and move our hearts by a faithful picturing of life. And the wonderful thing is how he endorses the inspired teaching of our Lord, by his supreme fidelity to fact.

I venture to say that when the literature of life finds itself in conflict with our Lord, when it leaves the impression that, if men are cautious, they can escape the penalties of sin, always that literature is shallow, and springs either from imperfect observation, or from designed and deliberate suppression of many of the facts of life.

When genius is faithful, as in Shakespeare it was supremely faithful ; when it has no theory to uphold, and no immorality to justify ; it ranges itself, unconsciously, and just because of its

fidelity, with Him who is the Faithful and True
Witness.

Again in the teaching of Jesus about man, we
mark the inwardness of His morality. It is not
that which goeth into a man which defileth him.

For our Lord the greatest of all troubles was
not the battle of a man with circumstance. It
was the unseen battle that is waged on the field
of his own heart. And nobody can study
Shakespeare without discovering in his tragedies
a like stern insistence on the inward.

He does not minimise the outward conflict,
any more than our blessed Lord did. One of the
dark elements in every tragedy lies in the pressure
of environment. But the grimmest conflict, the
one that holds us awed, is not the conflict with
environment. It is the conflict of the divided
heart.*

Hamlet was torn asunder inwardly, and that
inward division is the tragedy. The deadliest
combat of Othello was not with Iago but with
himself. Macbeth had many high and goodly
qualities. He had gifts of leadership and was a
constant lover ; and the battlefield of heaven

* So Antony, I, ii, 120-121 : 132.

and hell for him was in the shrouded places of his soul.

Shakespeare felt, just as our Lord felt, that the determinative field is inward. It is there men win the victories that matter most ; it is there they are most tragically beaten. And then added to that is this deep truth, so evident in Shakespeare, that true rewards and penalties are inward.

No pain from a sword-cut of Macduff is comparable to Macbeth's interior agonies. Cordelia dies for loving, but who does not feel the radiance of her soul ? Faithful to fact Shakespeare recognises the infinite significance of what is inward, and that is just what our blessed Saviour did.

Mark you, Shakespeare does not try to do it. I cannot sufficiently insist on that. He does not consciously try to square his tragedies with the gospel-teaching which he knew so well. Looking at life with an unbiassed eye, and supremely faithful to everything he saw, he finds himself ranged with the great Teacher.

I would note again that in our Lord's eyes the deadliest vices are the loveless ones. Wherever there was a touch of love, for the Master there was a ray of hope. I do not imply that He ever belittled evil, or took light views of sin ; only that in His judgment some sins were deadlier than others.

When the woman taken in sin was brought before Him, He refused to condemn her for her sins. It was on the hard and loveless Pharisees that He poured the vials of His condemnation. And it is notable that in the eyes of Shakespeare, as in the judgment of our Lord, the hard, cold vices are the worst.

In Shakespeare there is a world of pity for those who love not wisely but too well. They suffer, and reap as they have sown, but they are never hateful. It is the cold villainy of Iago, the ingratitude of Goneril and Regan—it is such things that are portrayed as damnable.

The strange thing is that the world's estimate is largely contrary to that of Jesus. Sins of passion it condemns ; the hard sins of the market it condones. On the one side stands the world : on the other side stands Christ. And Shakespeare is on the side of Christ.

Lastly, with our Lord every man is a potential child of God. His real affinity is not with evil ; his real affinity is with the good.

ON THE NATURE OF MAN

What a world of meaning is in the phrase that the prodigal "came to himself." That riotous and reckless evil-liver was not the real man at all. The real man was he who spurned his vices, and felt his kinship with the father, and longed for the good fellowship of home. The life of goodness was his native element—in that, he was at home : the life of riot brought him to starvation ; it was the highway to destruction. And though Shakespeare never preaches—he is far too great an artist to do that—nothing is more patent in his tragedies than the self-destructiveness of evil.

Evil not only disintegrates the world ; it rends and ruins and destroys the evil-doer. It wrecks his own life as well as that of others. It slays him as surely as his victims. All which is Shakespeare's way of showing us that man's true affinity is not with evil, but with goodness and with heaven and with God.

> Trailing clouds of glory do we come
> From God, who is our home.

Shakespeare has no doubt of that. The soul is poisoned in the air of evil, and therefore it was never meant to breathe it. Its native air is the upper air of heaven.

IV

ON THE WORTH OF WOMAN

NOTHING is more wonderful in Shakespeare than his gallery of noble women. In comedy and in tragedy alike we find ourselves moving in their company.

It has been said of Sir Walter Scott that he was too chivalrous to criticise women. If he does not strike deep into the female heart, it is because of a kind of gallant reverence. But Shakespeare is more wonderful than Scott, for he never hesitates to probe the deeps, and yet emerges with a faith in womanhood to which literature affords no parallel.

Shakespeare had companied with Lady Macbeth : he had dwelt deep with Goneril and Regan : he had explored the mystery of iniquity and suffered its full impression on his heart. And yet for him womanhood was beautiful—" enskied and sainted," human, yet a little lower than the angels.

54

ON THE WORTH OF WOMAN

We feel the wonder of this more when we remember that Shakespeare was a player, and as such would have little intercourse with the purest types of womanhood in England.

We all know that in Shakespeare's day women's parts were played by boys. Whether for better or for worse there were no actresses in the Elizabethan theatre.* But the standing of a player then was very different from what it is to-day—and Shakespeare was a player.

Sir Walter Scott had the entry to every circle in the land. He had a welcome everywhere ; he had the enriching friendship of the noblest women of his time. With Shakespeare it was different ; he was a player and doors were closed to him ; and yet he has given us a matchless portraiture of noble and heroic women.

It might be suggested that in so doing he was not painting from the life. Denied access to the womanhood of England, he drew on his imagination. But though all his women are imaginatively grasped—seen rather than studied—they impress one as intensely real.

* Cf.

> " I shall see
> Some squeaking Cleopatra boy my greatness."
> Antony and Cleopatra, V, ii, 219-220.

CHRIST IN SHAKESPEARE

The last thing one would say of Shakespeare's women is that they are fictions of the fancy. They are not too bright or good for human nature's daily food. They move along the cloudy ways of life, steadfast and clear-eyed, yet human real women to their finger-tips.

It is again worthy of remark that Shakespeare kept his ideals to the end. Whatever life may have brought him of the dark, he never altered in his view of womanhood.

It has been held that Shakespeare had his tragic period, when for him the sun and stars were darkened, when he was baffled by the weary weight of all this unintelligible world. But even then, in the day of his Iagos, he had his vision of Desdemona. Even then, amid the agonies of Lear, he held to the pure, true spirit of Cordelia.

Life oftens leaves men with wrecked ideals; the enthusiast becomes the cynic. The hard, bitter teaching of experience shows the feet of clay in what was worshipped once. But life left Shakespeare with Miranda, a conception nobler and more lovely than we ever find in his comedies of youth.

ON THE WORTH OF WOMAN

Some men cling to their ideals. They hold to them desperately in the deepening shadows. Shakespeare never would suggest to me a man who is clinging to a spar amid the wreckage. Faithful to fact and to himself, in the darkest period of his life, he has emerged to where the sun is shining and the blue heaven is above us all.

Miranda is not a last attempt to make shore on broken pieces of the ship. Miranda is the last discovery of one who has gone sounding on his perilous way. With a supreme fidelity Shakespeare fronted life, under a heaven " with which we cannot cope," and what was noble and beautiful remained.

Students will note that Shakespeare was no believer in the inferiority of woman. His heroines are intensely feminine, yet they stand on an equality with men.

Dickens seems to have found his ideal of woman in the gentle clinging type. Shakespeare's only woman of this type is the ineffectual Ophelia. To him woman was a noble comrade, ministering not by weakness but by strength, and in her strength an inspiration.

In the region of the will, Lady Macbeth was far

from inferior to her husband. In the region of the intellect, Portia was a match for any man. In courage, in constancy, in " grave and errorless purpose " the heroines of Shakespeare stand supreme, the loyal and equal helpers of the heroes.

One wonders where Shakespeare got this exalted thought of womanhood. Most certainly he did not get it from his predecessors in the English drama. He may have got it from his mother, as men very generally do ; but unquestionably the final source was Christ.

Whatever else our Lord did, He immeasurably exalted womanhood. I can understand a man not being a Christian ; I can never understand a woman. And just as Shakespeare in his view of man betrays the uplifting touch of Christ, so he does in his portraiture of woman.

Christ knew Salome and Herodias, just as Shakespeare knew Goneril and Regan. Christ was familiar with the frightful things that may be hidden in the heart of womanhood. Yet knowing the worst He found in womanhood something nobler than the world had dreamed of. And again Shakespeare follows in His steps.

58

ON THE WORTH OF WOMAN

With him woman is not a piece of property, nor a plaything for hours of relaxation. She is a brave, clear-eyed, resourceful being, capable of the finest and the best. In will, in intellect, in steadfastness, in sacrifice, unsurpassed by man, though "without him not to be made perfect."

For Shakespeare ideal womanhood is never a woman of the ascetic type. He "enskies" her, but never "unsexes" her, to use the word of Lady Macbeth.

Shakespeare had no quarrel with sex. He accepted life, and found it "very good." He had no sympathy with such as find in sex "the great original mistake of the Creator." He knew, just as Byron did, that

> Man's love is of man's life a thing apart,
> 'Tis woman's whole existence.

It is through love, invariably, that Shakespeare's heroines "arrive." It is love that liberates their powers, and changes the child into the woman. Desdemona, "a maiden never bold," grows fearless and confronts her world, not because she is clamouring for liberty, but because she loves Othello.

Shakespeare hates all prudery ; he has no

patience with ascetic virtue. He sees as clearly as the new psychology that prudery conceals the opposite. And yet such is the balance and sanity of Shakespeare that no moralist ever proclaimed more eloquently that the sensuous infinite is a delusion.

Juliet, Portia, Desdemona never attempt to root out what is basic. For them what is basic is not base. But Cleopatra makes the huge mistake of disordering life's interests, and the appointed end of that is tragedy. Cleopatra puts first what should be last. She subordinates everything to sense. For her rich and restless nature she seeks satisfaction in the sensuous. And the terrific moral lesson of her so disordered life is that the sensuous infinite is a delusion.

In all this we are again reminded of the teaching of the Master. He does not demand asceticism ; He demands the ordering of interests. He says " Seek ye first the kingdom "—give the first place to what is spiritual—and all else shall be added unto you.

Most of the tragedies in life spring from the disordering of interests, from putting last what should be first, and first what should be last.

And the Christlike thing about the heroines of Shakespeare is that, unlike Egypt's harlot, they never make that tragical mistake.

They recognise that the whole of human nature is to be received with thanksgiving. They recognise that all that God has dowered us with, is given us richly to enjoy. But they put first things first—they seek the kingdom first—with pure and resolute will they order life into a beautiful and harmonious whole.

They do not extinguish ; they subordinate. They keep down, instead of crushing out. Their eye is not sensual but single, and therefore their whole bodies are full of light. That is why Shakespeare's heroines are charming, as rich in attraction as in redemptive power, and the good and guiding angels of the heroes.

For as Ruskin has told us in a noble passage, it is the heroines in the plays who are the saviours. It is through women that redemption comes if it comes at all.

It is Portia who saves from Shylock and, so doing, averts catastrophe. In Lear there is no hope at all save in the loving ardour of Cordelia. But for the wild recklessness of Romeo, Juliet's stratagem would have succeeded, and love would have been crowned in happiness.

Shakespeare's heroines do not stand alone : their lives are bound up with the lives of men. They are the lovers, the guardians, and the guides of those in whose service they find liberty. When they are good their influence for good is the biggest thing a man can know ; when they are evil, their influence is death.

For we must never forget how deeply Shakespeare felt the hateful influence of a bad woman. His passionate reverence for woman was emphatically not the child of blindness.

But for Lady Macbeth, Duncan would never have been murdered. Whatever the dark ambitions of her husband, he was not the stuff that murderers are made of. He was too full of the milk of human kindness ; he let " I dare not wait upon I would " ; his loyalty might not have held him from the deed, but certainly his imagination would. But Lady Macbeth was always at his side, and he loved her and tremendously admired her. Unimaginative, single-purposed, she screwed his courage to the sticking point. No man could have wrought upon Macbeth as this dreadful but loving woman did. For him she was the procuress of hell.

At the other pole of evil stands Cleopatra, selfish, sensual, conscienceless ; glowing with a magnetic attractiveness, dazzling in variety and charm ; to a man like Antony quite irresistible in the glamour of her sensuous witchery, and yet steadily drawing him to make his bed in hell.

Antony never really loved her as Macbeth unquestionably loved his wife. He was too critical to be really in love ; with his better judgment he suspected her. I do not think, spite of Enobarbus, that he ever ceased to think her cunning ; for him she was always the serpent of old Nile.

There was a vulgar and coarse strain in her. She could storm like a virago. It marks the perfect fidelity of Shakespeare that he never dreams of hiding this—a woman who lived in and for sensation, utterly and absolutely selfish, an actress because she could not help it.

Men do not love such women ; what they think love is fascination. Give it what name you will, the craving for them is a sensual craving. And nothing more magnificently illustrates the moral severity of Shakespeare than the way in which a woman such as this spells ruin for the nobility of manhood.

Lascivious writers would have cloaked all that. Shakespeare never cloaks it. Inexorably and remorselessly he conducts Antony to misery and suicide. The lights go out—the music ceases—the laughter dies—the glory passes, because a man has yielded, through a woman, to the lust of the flesh and of the eye.

The glory of Shakespeare is that he instils that terror without the slightest attempt at any moral teachings. Moralists would never have felt as he felt the sensuous witchery of Cleopatra. In his perfect fidelity to life he disguises nothing, and distorts nothing, and yet at the end " the dead are there, and her guests are in the depths of hell."

No young heart can say of Shakespeare, " Oh he does not understand." He does not sit apart in cold austerity frowning on the thrilling of the senses. He joins in the revels of the prodigal, but he sees perfectly what the prodigal is blind to, that ruin is coming, and remorse, and the husks that the swine do eat.

Shakespeare was no reformer : he was a child

of the Renaissance. But he did what no one else in England did, he moralised the Renaissance. He took life in its glory and its fulness, and shot it through with heaven and hell, and with the steady beat of inexorable law.

But Shakespeare does more than show us the power of women in the life of men. He shows us what an infinite loss it is to men never to have known a good and noble woman.

One feels how different life would have been to Hamlet if he could have had Portia for a friend. A brave, clear-eyed, noble woman would have made all the difference for Hamlet. It was part of the tragedy of Hamlet that such a woman never crossed his path, nor offered him the service of her love.

Of the two women who moved within his sphere, one was an incestuous mother. Just where he was prepared to love and reverence, he found treachery and bestiality. And the shock to a nature such as his of discovering what his mother really was, was a mighty factor in his ruined life. A noble mother ennobles all womanhood. She is an anchor cast within the veil. No one whose mother has had a noble soul can say "frailty, thy name is woman." One of the sources of Hamlet's wretched failure to deal with life in the victorious way, was the absence from his life of noble motherhood.

The other woman was Ophelia, and Ophelia was weak and ineffectual. She was a wistful, gentle, timid little thing, without initiative or resource. She was one to be cherished in all tenderness, and treated as a child, and sheltered from the battlings of the world. Ophelia was incapable of understanding Hamlet, and so was incapable of helping him. He knew that if he bared his heart to her she would be terrified, and run and tell Polonius. And while this gentle, clinging, timid kind of woman is often as a downy nest for weariness, she is rarely helpful in the storm.

Had it been Juliet or Desdemona, the story of Hamlet would have had a different issue. Love would have cleared his vision; it would have braced his will, and purified his soul. The tragedy of Hamlet had its roots, not only in the flaws of his own character, but also in the absence from his life of lofty and ennobling womanhood.

Nothing could more clearly show what woman meant to Shakespeare. Never to have loved a noble woman was one of his avenues to tragedy.

And when we add to that the long roll of his heroines who are rich in guiding and redemptive power, we begin to feel the wonder of it all.

Here Shakespeare is not the child of the Renaissance. He is the follower of Christ. His standard of values is not Florentine; it is pre-eminently Christian. It breathes the spirit of One who in the home at Nazareth saw every day the wonder of true womanhood, and never lost that wonder to the end.

V

ON THE FACT OF TEMPTATION

(MACBETH)

TEMPTATION is one of the universal elements in human life. It is an experience which nobody escapes. One may escape the experience of illness, and never know the perils of poverty or wealth : but temptation is a fact in every life, never to be eluded. It is, as Thackeray says, a most obsequious servant, and will follow a man into the loneliest desert, as readily as it will follow him to church.

Character depends, in no small measure, on a man's reaction to temptation. There are no issues in life so determinative as the issues of conflict with temptation. And this conflict is one of the constant elements in all the greater tragedies of life, as it is in the greater tragedies of literature.

No writer equals Shakespeare in profound and penetrating studies of temptation. Of these there is none more absorbing than Macbeth. I shall try to elucidate some of the salient features in the temptation of Macbeth, as it presented itself to the mind of Shakespeare.

In the first place in the temptation of Macbeth there was solicitation from without. The play begins with the witches (I, i).

One should note that these witches are just witches. They are evil, repulsive, bearded (I, iii, 46) women. They are neither furies nor fates. They are human beings who traffic with the devil. In the time of Shakespeare the belief in witches was well-nigh universal, and no one in the audience had the slightest difficulty in recognising these disgusting hags.

Nobody would dream that they were symbolical, representing what lay hidden in Macbeth's own mind. As a matter of fact they do not do that, either in the first or second apparition ; for in the first they call Macbeth Thane of Cawdor, an eventuality he had never dreamed of ; and in the second they buoy him up with hopes which otherwise could never have been his (IV, i).

The witches are Shakespeare's medium for

conveying solicitation from without, a medium no seventeenth century audience would ever dream of laughing at. And one feels the sublimity of Shakespeare's genius in this, that he so paints the witches in foul and dusky awfulness, that though belief in witchcraft has departed, nobody feels like laughing at them yet.

It has been argued that in the first appearing there is no "supernatural soliciting" at all— although the phrase is Macbeth's own (I, iii, 130). The witches, it is said, simply state facts. They announce that which is going to be. They do not urge Macbeth to any action. They never suggest murder. But surely it is poor psychology to deny all suggestive influence to predictive and prophetic statement.

Men have been known to die on the date which was predicted for their death. In such prediction it might be true to say there was no soliciting to die. Yet such a prophecy, haunting the mind, and weakening the powers of resistance, un- questionably has a suggestive power that makes mysteriously for accomplishment.

So was it with the witches. Their predictions were solicitations. The statements they made

70

about the future gave to the mind of Macbeth a bent and bias. And all this the more surely because of his belief that witches were granted, by the powers of darkness, glimpses of futurity.*

What then does Shakespeare mean by this kind of solicitation from without ? It seems to me there is a good deal of loose talk on that matter.

Critics talk about external evil as though evil was a force like gravitation. They speak of the momentum of evil in the world pressing in upon the soul. But there is no moral evil in the scheme of things. The only possible external pressure is that exercised by personalities.

It is not fashionable to believe in the devil now ; and in view of popular conceptions of the devil that is scarcely to be wondered at. But that there is some mighty and malign intelligence, who organises and controls the powers of darkness ; that we wrestle not with flesh and blood, but with principalities and powers, this, the belief of Jesus, seems to me entirely philosophic, and alone adequate to account for many of the phenomena of human life and history.

* A similar " supernatural soliciting " may be found in the Old Testament. Elisha says to Hazael, " The Lord hath shewed me that thou shalt be king over Syria." Here is a prophetic statement. There is no hint of murder. Yet the next day Hazael smothers the king.—2 Kings viii, 7-15.

We are all tempted from without, as Macbeth was tempted from without. So cunning and timely are these solicitations that they suggest not a force but an intelligence. For force works blindly, and is unvarying, and is never deftly nor delicately personal, as the solicitings of evil always are.

But besides the witches there was another external influence leading Macbeth into temptation. It was the solicitation of his wife.

Few characters in literature have impressed the popular imagination as Lady Macbeth has done. Students have tried to gather what she looked like, but in vain. If " this little hand " (V, i, 58) hints that she was little, her gentlewoman refers to her " dignity of body " (V, i, 62), where the suggestion leans to the other side.

Lady Macbeth, whatever she may be, is not an utterly callous woman. A careful reading of the play makes that evident. She has to pray to be unsexed (I, v, 42) ; she needs wine to make her bold (II, ii, 1) ; she cannot slay Duncan for he is like her father (II, ii, 12-14) ; after the murder she cannot bear the darkness (V, i, 25-27). And the awful revelation of her sleep-walking betrays a nature different in the deeps from that of an utterly heartless, callous woman.

She was a woman of an indomitable will, who never let " I dare not " wait upon " I would." She had far less imagination than her husband, for Macbeth was of " imagination all compact." She saw intensely but not imaginatively ; she thought that " a little water " would put all things right (II, ii, 67) ; she failed to picture the remorse and agony that would make bloodstains burn like fire.

Macbeth not only admires her (I, vii, 73-75) ; he loves her devotedly and tenderly. He calls her " my dearest love " (I, v, 58) ; he addresses her as " dearest chuck " (III, ii, 45). Macbeth, then, is tempted from without not only by malignant powers of darkness ; he is tempted also by his dearest.

So was Jesus tempted by Simon Peter. So is many a man tempted. It has been said that when the devil wants to snare an Englishman he generally does it through his wife and children. One of the hardest things to do in life is to say to those we love and who love us, " Get thee behind me, Satan."

But if the play exhibits solicitation from without, it also exhibits, with an equal clearness, that such solicitation is powerless unless it finds an answering chord within.

There is no suggestion in the drama that wife or witches forced Macbeth. He never, even in his wildest moods, shifts responsibility to them. They struck a chord which was already vibrating. They added fuel to a kindled fire. They gave form to dim and formless things, already lurking and stirring in his soul.

Why did he " start " when he heard the witches' prophecies (I, iii, 51) ? Banquo heard them entirely unmoved. Why instantly did he betray fear (I, iii, 51) ? Why was he " rapt " (I, iii, 56) as men are in revelations ? To Macbeth this was a revelation, not of the hell without him but of the hell within him, where already, unseen by any eye, there were movings towards things he dare not name.

Within four and twenty hours of the apparition, he says

> Stars, hide your fires,
> Let not light see my black and deep desires.
> (I, iv, 51.)

Such dark and deep desires were never formed

74

and fashioned in a day. They were in the heart, like chords attuned and vibrating, when the witches unrolled the curtain of the future.

In other words, when the play opens, Macbeth is in unstable equilibrium. And always, when there is unstable equilibrium, the devil has his opportunity.

Had Macbeth been resolute for good, the witches might have spared their pains. Had he been set on evil with an iron will, their intervention would have been unnecessary. Lady Macbeth never sees any witches. It was his wavering and undecided will that gave the powers of hell their opportunity. It was not the witches nor his wife that ruined Macbeth. His ruin was his character.

Note how he says, " We will speak further " (I, v, 72), when Lady Macbeth insists upon the murder. It is a touch of a profound significance, and Shakespeare meant it to be so. He will not close with the thought of murdering Duncan; but no more will he banish the dark thought— and that unstable equilibrium spelled ruin.

When a train is drawing towards a station, a man may say, " I can't decide if I will get out here." He swithers : he is irresolute ; he cannot make up his mind. Meanwhile the train has stopped, and started, and the man is being carried forward by it. Not to decide is to decide against.

There are many problems that confront us in this life, where decision is not necessary. It is sometimes wise to keep an open mind. But there are moral and spiritual issues which cannot be escaped by indecision. Indecision in these is itself choice.

So was it with Macbeth. There was a great deal that was good in him. He was brave ; he loved his wife ; he felt the nobleness of loyalty and honour. But he was in unstable equilibrium. He never cried, " Get thee behind me, Satan." He dallied where he should have resisted ; he " talked further " where he should have shut his ears ; and so, like Judas, he went to his own place.

We should note, too, how Macbeth's temptation met him in the day of his success. That is the first thing which he mentions in the letter which he writes his wife (I, v, 1).

There had been a rebellion of the Western clans, and Macbeth had victoriously dealt with that. Hard on the heels of it came another peril—an invasion by the King of Norway. And Macbeth, undaunted and unwearied, had flung himself on the invader, and forced him to humiliating terms.

Flushed with that double victory, which had made him the saviour of his country, he is now marching towards Forres, to report on matters to the king. And *then*, in the hour of triumph, when he had proved his genius and saved his land, the witches met him on the heath.

There are temptations, known to all of us, peculiar to the hour of failure. Men are tempted in the hour of failure to fall back on things they have forsworn. Men are often tempted, when they fail, to seize at low and immediate satisfactions, not infrequently those of sensuality.

To lose heart and to grow bitter ; to begrudge others their success ; to take up a quarrel with the world ; to forfeit the sunshine of the love of God, these, too, are insidious temptations that haunt the melancholy hour of failure. But other temptations, not less insidious, strike at men in the hour of success.

Success is always apt to dim the grandeur of the moral law. A man in the hour of magnificent success is prone to think he is above morality.

77

Restrictions are meant for common people; conquering genius is above restriction; no one has the right to legislate for it.

The hour of triumph is just as hard to bear as the hour of humiliation and defeat. Success, no less than failure, has its doors that open on to hell. Had Macbeth been beaten by Macdonwald the witches would never have appeared to him. They met him in the hour of his success.

Lastly we are to note that temptation met Macbeth along the line of his dominating passion. His ruling passion was ambition (I, vii, 25-8) and it was through his ambition that temptation struck.

Had Macbeth been a man of easy temper, content to live and die a general; had his nature really been " luxurious " as Malcolm thought it was (IV, iii, 58), the witches, though they might have met him, would never have addressed him as they did. They appealed to the passion that was strongest in him; to the most powerful craving of his being; to the dreams and visions of his soul.

With Othello it was different. He was tempted in unexpected ways. Jealousy seemed alien from Othello. Tempted there, he was taken by surprise. But Macbeth was not taken by surprise, nor assailed from an unlikely quarter. He was struck at through the passion of his soul.

So was it with our blessed Lord, when He was tempted with the vision of the kingdoms. Satan knew that the passion of His soul was to be Master of the kingdoms of the world. But He, in perfect poise with God, imperiously rejected the short-cut, and took the long and lonely way to final sovereignty.

Short-cuts are not God's. Neither Israel nor Christ was led that way. One of the subtlest temptations of the human soul is to outstrip God in its ambitions. Along that avenue Macbeth was tempted, and being tempted, fell ; and we say with Othello, " O, the pity of it."

VI

ON THE PERIL OF DELAY

(HAMLET)

MORE has been written about Hamlet than about any other character in literature, and even yet there is no agreement in the interpretation of his character.

Shakespeare worked long over the play, and his own conception may have altered. With the carelessness of genius, he may have allowed contradictions to stand. But it is not such contradictions that form the mystery of Hamlet. It is rather the richness of his character.

All life surprises us by its incalculable elements, and there is no character in literature richer in this incalculable element. That is why Hamlet lives, and is intensely real, and fascinates, and yet is so very hard to understand.

Now when the ghost appears to Hamlet and

reveals the murder of his father, we must first remember Hamlet's words :

> Haste me to know't, that I, with wings as swift
> As meditation or the thoughts of love
> May sweep to my revenge.
>
> (I, v, 29-31.)

There you have the mood to be expected in the heart of an adoring son ; for the love of Hamlet for his father is something without parallel in Shakespeare. And yet for all his love, and his horror, and his blazing indignation, to sweep to his revenge is the one thing Hamlet does not do.

He recognises the duty of revenge, and yet postpones the execution of it. He procrastinates ; he dallies ; he lets the weeks slip on with nothing done. This is not a tragedy of passion like Othello and Macbeth. It is a tragedy of delayed obedience. Two questions emerge which we must try to answer. (1) What lay at the back of this delay ? and (2) What effects did it produce ?

It is worth noting that had you asked Hamlet why he so delayed, you would have found him incapable of answering. In one of his monologue he dwells on that, and replies to his own soul

" I do not know " (IV, iv, 43). Macbeth was perfectly aware why he followed a certain line of action. Othello, at any moment, could have explained and justified himself. Hamlet, for all his gifts of intellect, and his faculty of intro-spection, is quite unable to understand himself.

Probably we are to find a hint in that of his extraordinary complexity of nature. Is it any wonder that he has baffled others, when he was a baffling problem to himself ? Probably, too, there is a hint in it of larger forces playing on his life, and making him unconsciously their instru-ment. Most men discern the hand of Heaven in the tasks and duties that they try to do. Hamlet discovered larger powers at work in his failure to do anything. It was because he was a riddle to himself that he recognised that more than self was moving in the hidden deep places of the soul.

First of all, then, taking the matter negatively, we are able to say with perfect confidence, that the strange and tragical delay of Hamlet was not due to any external causes.

There is not, I think, a hint in the whole play that the commanded duty was impossible.

Hamlet never alleges that excuse, never suggests that the deed is beyond his powers, nor would the ghost have urged him to a duty which he could not possibly discharge.

When Laertes hears of his father's death, he "sweeps on to his revenge." Had the king been guilty of the murder, all the Swiss guards could not have saved him. And if Laertes had stood in Hamlet's shoes, revenge would have been swift and sure, and the tragedy of delayed obedience unwritten.

Circumstance has its place in Shakespeare, just as it has its place in life. But it was not any external circumstance that opposed and baffled Hamlet. For that baffling we must seek deeper, in the intricacies of the soul; not in the realm of Denmark, but in the realm within.

With equal assurance we may lay it down that the delay did not spring from fear. Shakespeare is at special pains to show that Hamlet was no coward.

He was beloved of the people, and cowards are very rarely that. He had the touch of royalty about him, and in the common judgment was qualified for kingship. One could not conceive

Horatio, that antique Roman and most gallant heart, having a coward as his dearest friend.

He was no coward who shook off his friends, and insisted on following the beckoning ghost ; who fought with Laertes in the grave ; who was the first to board the pirate-ship. Whatever lay behind Hamlet's inaction it certainly was not any fear of death, for he was half in love with easeful death already.

Was it then the prickings of his conscience that held him back from action ? For the story, a heathen one originally, has been set by Shakespeare in a Christian atmosphere.

To that I can only reply that in the play I find no traces in the breast of Hamlet of a conscience uneasy and unsatisfied. Conscience holds him back from suicide, but it never holds him back from action. It deals with the question " To be or not to be," but never with " To do or not to do." Hamlet had not a shadow of a doubt that to revenge his father was his duty, and that in the shirking of it he was guilty.

We must not import into these far-off days the enlightened conscience of the twentieth century. There is no hint that he brooded on the words "Vengeance is mine, I will repay, saith the Lord." The passionate instincts of his filial heart cried out that his duty was revenge, and the voice from the other world proclaimed it also.

With opportunities daily in his power, with courage equal to his problem, unvisited by any pangs of conscience, miserable in inactivity, how are we to explain this strange delay, that forms the substance of the tragedy, and lies at the heart of the mystery of Hamlet?

I begin by citing some words of Hamlet which occur in a soliloquy, and which seem to me exceedingly important :

> Now, whether it be
> Bestial oblivion, or some craven scruple
> Of thinking too precisely on the event
> . . . I do not know.
> (IV, iv, 39-43.)

That is to say Hamlet was conscious that with him it was temperamental to think too precisely on the event.

That means that instead of acting, he was prone to set action in the light of thought. It was his habit to meditate and generalise rather than immediately to do a thing. All action implies limitation, and Hamlet with his subtle mind preferred the unlimited freedom of reflection, to the limitation inherent in a deed.

In Amiel, a man of our own time, that tendency is very clearly seen. He, too, had a philosophic mind of extraordinary power and subtlety. And like Hamlet, though in other respects he bears no resemblance to him, Amiel shrank from the limiting of action.

The question is, would we gather from the play that Hamlet was a man of that kind ? Was he given to brooding and to generalising ? Did he suffer from excess of thought ? I think there can be no question about that.

For instance, after the ghost has vanished what is the first thing Hamlet does ? He draws out his tablets to make a note of it, that a man may smile, and smile, and be a villain (I, v, 97). Laertes would have drawn his sword ; he would have swept on to vengeance there and then. Hamlet does not draw his sword ; he draws his tablets. He is already more concerned to note a truth than to slay the murderer of his father. Duty is forgotten in reflection.

So when he hears the shouts of revelry, he begins

to brood on the drunkenness of Denmark. When he sees the skulls thrown from the grave, at once his imagination catches fire. Laertes would have unpacked his heart by swift and determinative deeds. Hamlet " unpacked his heart with words."

To such a nature action is repugnant, especially action with enormous consequences. These consequences give such food for thought that the brain becomes preternaturally active. Hamlet knew that in his commanded duty the whole commonwealth of Denmark was involved :

> The time is out of joint ; O cursed spite,
> That ever I was born to set it right !

A simple duty he might have done at once, spite of his proneness to undue reflection. But this duty, with its staggering consequences, overthrew the balance of his being. The boundless consequences of his commanded action so wrought upon his brain, that in trying to exhaust them speculatively, his sword remained undrawn.

One should note carefully that this state of mind is very different from that of indecision. Hamlet was not a vulgar waverer, cursed with instability of will.

It is not uncommon to meet people who can't

make up their mind. They are swayed to this side and to that ; they are irresolute and undecided. But whatever Hamlet was, he was not unstable, incapable of resolution, weak and useless because always wavering.

His swift resolve to settle with the ghost ; his sudden piercing of the arras with his sword ; his determination to utilise the players ; his substitution of his own for the king's letter, such things do not suggest the weakling, unstable and infirm of purpose.

Hamlet's delayed obedience has a nobler root. It springs not from want of will but from excess of thought. It is akin to the spirit that does nothing in its craving for an impossible perfection. It is the malady of the man who sees so clearly, or is so eager for a perfect vision, that he fails, amid the half-lights of this world, to do the duty that is appointed him.

In all action there are risks, and we are here to take these risks. We walk by faith not sight ; we have all to take our leaps into the dark. Men may fail to do so through sheer weakness, but Hamlet was not cowardly like that. With him the " native hue of resolution " was "sicklied o'er with the pale cast of thought."

ON THE PERIL OF DELAY

And then one notes that this tremendous duty confronted Hamlet in his hour of darkness. He was already stupefied with a terrific shock, when he first heard the summons of the ghost.

Often in an overwhelming sorrow men become incapable of acting. Things lose their eagerness and their charm. The zest of life is gone. And in the very season of his call, which might have taxed the height of vigour, Hamlet was smitten in some such way as that.

Before the ghost appeared to him, before he knew his father had been murdered, Hamlet is already sick of life and brooding upon suicide. His world has fallen into ruins, and life has lost its lustre for him, by the incestuous marriage of his mother.

Often, when men lose faith in one person, they lose faith in everything. When one soul tragically fails us, the sun and moon and stars are darkened. And the awful failure of his mother, the revelation of her shallow worthlessness, meant for Hamlet, in the shock of it, the crushing of his universe.

Whether the temperament of Hamlet, in normal circumstances, would have swept on to its revenge, is a question that we need not raise, for Shakespeare does not raise it. The drama turns on an overwhelming task given to one to whom action was repugnant, and given in the very hour when that repugnancy was overpowering.

And then, added to that, there was the haunting fear lest the ghost might be the instrument of darkness. " The spirit that I have seen may be the devil " (II, ii, 628).

To a brooding nature such as Hamlet's, such doubts were certain to present themselves. If his loved mother had deceived him, might not the ghost deceive him also ? If his mother's love had been a sham, her marriage-faithfulness a hideous mockery, was it not possible that the unearthly vision had been trafficking in mockery as well ?

The frightful revelation of his mother had made Hamlet feel that deception might be anywhere. He could not trust his eyes, when once they had been so horribly tricked. And though the doubt, in itself, might not be enough to stay him from revenge, it would play steadily on his reluctancy.

Nearer than that, perhaps, we cannot get to the mystery of Hamlet, though one feels, when that is said, that there is much that is still unsaid. We see his brooding, over-reflective temperament forced by shock into the misery of scepticism, and perhaps beyond that we cannot go.

ON THE PERIL OF DELAY

So we pass to the second enquiry—What results flowed from this delayed obedience ?

And first we watch how steadily and surely it took the joy and colour out of life. Hamlet, spite of all his swift excitements, is a profoundly melancholy being. " It is no matter," he says sadly ; he lived in a world where nothing seemed to matter. In the gloom that came down and settled on him, he came perilously near to madness, and probably some dim consciousness of that guided him to play the part of lunacy.

Whenever he acts on overmastering impulse, you at once detect a change of spirit. He grows alert and interested. The clouds break ; he is actually gleeful. But his prevailing temper, in inaction, is strangely different from that, and he moves on the margins of despair.

There is a profound and abiding truth in that. Let anybody shirk his duty, no matter for what reason ; let him dally, and refuse to come to grips, with the task that has been given him, and always the sun darkens, and joy goes, and all the thrill of life, and the clouds return after the rain.

Shakespeare is not disparaging the life of

thought, nor is he pitiless to the shattered spirit. He only shows what inevitably follows when duty lies undone. Melancholy deepens ; life grows worthless ; intensity of interest vanishes ; the man grows " half in love with easeful death."

Bunyan tells us that his pilgrims crossed the stile into Bypath Meadow. The meadow doubtless was very easy going, and the highway was flinty to the feet. But it was Bypath Meadow, and just because of that it brought the travellers to Doubting Castle, and to the grim clutch of Giant Despair.

Again how clearly is it written for us that through inaction there is no escape. There are greater possibilities of harm in doing nothing than in attempting to do what is demanded.

Had Hamlet swept to his revenge the king would have forfeited his life. Probably that would have been the only death, and no one would have been brokenhearted over it. Such was the popularity of Hamlet, and his favour with the populace, that he would have been set on the throne with acclamation.

Had he acted swiftly he would have taken risks, for in all action we take risks ; but how grimly does Shakespeare show that he took greater risks in doing nothing—consider what emerges in the play.

Polonius dies, stabbed through the arras. Ophelia loses her reason and is drowned. Laertes dies of the poisoned sword, which had been tinctured for his adversary. Rosencrantz and Guildenstern go to their doom in England. The Queen is poisoned, and the King is slain—and all the fruits of Hamlet's inactivity.

Not to decide may seem innocuous, but in this mysterious life it is never that. It involves others, and tangles up their lives, in ways that sometimes seem incredible. We talk of " living dangerously," but no man lives more dangerously than the man who dallies with his duty.

And then, and with this I close, Hamlet destroyed himself. He lies dead on the stage that holds the ghastliness of the other corpses.

Had he swept on to his revenge, his own life would have been in little danger. He was the people's darling, and the people would have seen to it that no harm should befall him. His delayed obedience spelled death for others, but the crowning tragedy is this, that it spelled death for himself also.

Now it is one of the great messages of Shakespeare that evil is self-destructive, and therefore out of harmony with the moral order of the universe. What Hamlet enforces is that this grim consequence not only dogs the heels of positive evil, but of negative evil as well.

Hamlet is not an active wrong-doer. His criminality is doing nothing. Hamlet has a noble heart and loves all noble things—there is a world between him and Macbeth. Yet his inaction, his negative resistance to the moral order of the world, is as fatal as the most daring criminality. Evil is self-destructive, and evil is more than action. Inaction under a ringing moral challenge may itself be immorality. All which Shakespeare knew, and portrays with such perfect fidelity to fact, that when we close the book we whisper " I'll go pray " (I, v, 132).

VII

ON THE POWER OF CHOICE

(MERCHANT OF VENICE)

THIS play was probably written in the year 1596, and though the great comedies and tragedies were still to come then, the dramatist was no longer immature.

Not only were some of his Histories already written, and several of his lighter Comedies, but he had already risen to the tragic power of Romeo and Juliet.

This is the first great comedy, in the sense that it is a comedy of character. Its abiding interest is not amusing incident; it is the display and development of character. Even in laughter, says Solomon, the heart is sorrowful; and through all the laughter of the play, the heart is moved with sorrow by the tragic character of Shylock.

One notes wonderingly the perfect skill with which the strands of interest are inwoven. There is no necessary connection between the pound of flesh, and the caskets, and the comedy of the rings. Yet Shakespeare, perfecting what others had attempted, blends the three stories into such a unity, that the reader is unconscious of their frontiers.

Even the clown, Launcelot Gobbo, helps in this, by passing from the service of Shylock to that of Bassanio. His exchange of masters is a subtle touch in the unifying of the elements. The clowns of Shakespeare, like the clowns of life, have larger purposes to serve than they themselves have the least conception of.

The story of the caskets, in one form or other, is one of the old stories of the world. It is found for instance in the Gesta Romanorum. Shakespeare's version of the tale is this :

A wealthy Italian, whose home is Belmont, a fair estate near Venice, in his will, made just before his death (I, ii, 30) leaves instructions about his daughter's marriage. She is not at liberty to choose a husband at the bidding of her heart. Three caskets are fashioned, one of gold, one of silver, one of lead. In one of the three, concealed, is the portrait of Portia. And he, and he alone, who chooses the casket which contains the portrait, is to be the husband of Portia.

The only guidance given to the suitors is the sibylline motto which each bears. The gold one has the inscription, " Who chooseth me shall gain what many men desire." The silver one, " Who chooseth me shall get as much as he deserves." The lead one, " Who chooseth me must give and hazard all he hath." And the penalty of choosing wrongly is that the wooer immediately departs, and remains to the end of his life unwedded (II, i, 40).

Suitors from every quarter flock to Belmont, one of them from Scotland (I, ii, 83). All of them, with three exceptions, learning the terms, decline to put their fortunes to the test. The three exceptions are the Prince of Morocco, who selects the gold casket ; the Prince of Arragon, who selects the silver ; Bassanio of Venice who selects the lead, and so doing, finds the portrait, and wins Portia.

One could not conceive a modern father restricting his daughter's liberty like that. Nor could one conceive a modern daughter tolerating such restrictions of her rights. But two things must be borne in mind.

The first is that when this story was first told, the *patria potestas* was far greater than it is to-day.

The second is that when the story was first told, the hand of heaven was recognised in such things. Great actions were determined by the chance opening of Vergil or the Bible. "The lot is cast into the lap, but the whole ordering thereof is of the Lord."

So I am led to speak a little on the important theme of choosing. But first I should like to make it clear what a large element of necessity there is in life.

Portia's marriage was necessitated; it lay beyond the compass of her will. And we shall never rightly view life till we remember that there is in every life that necessary element.

A man may choose his bride, but he does not choose his father or his mother. He does not choose the home in which he spends his tender and impressionable years. He does not choose his country, nor the religion of his early childhood, nor the talents and gifts peculiarly his own.

Such elements of life lie quite beyond the will.

ON THE POWER OF CHOICE

We do not of our free choice embrace them.
They are imposed on us by external forces, over
which we have no control. And yet their
influence on happiness and opportunity, not less
than on character, are profound, unceasing, and
tremendous.

On no reasonable view of life can it be held
that they decide our *fate*. But they certainly
decide our *trial*. We know that the issue of the
fight is in our own hands, for the sense of
responsibility is real. But on what field the
battle shall be fought, and who shall be the
deadliest enemies, and at what points in the long
conflict the aid of heaven will be needed most,
all that is largely determined for a man by things
beyond the compass of his choice.

Here it may be well to say a word on the old
and vexed question of free-will. How can anyone
be really free to choose, if the Almighty foreknows
and foreordains ? To postulate free-will seems
to abrogate divine fore-knowledge. To deny
divine fore-knowledge is " to limit the Holy One
of Israel." And men all down the ages have
debated the deep question, can these opposites
be reconciled ?

Now life and conduct assume the fact of freedom. All law rests on its reality. Our blessed Lord assumed the fact of freedom : " Ye will not come to me that ye might have life." To deny therefore the fact of human freedom in the supposed interests of God, is dishonouring to life, and it is disloyal to Jesus.

Must I then yield up divine fore-knowledge ? Must I send it whistling down the wind ? It seems to me far wiser to say quietly, " now we know in part." Life is rich in unresolved antinomies, insoluble to thought, but all perfectly soluble in practice. " We went through fire and water," says the psalmist ; through things contradictory to one another. And through such opposites we go in life,—we go, though we cannot understand. It is wise to remember that we have finite minds, and that things irreconcilable to us, may lie, in perfect harmony, in the infinite intelligence of God.

To come back to our play. We recognise in the story of the caskets the strange significance of life's lesser choices.

To choose a golden instead of a leaden casket, or a leaden instead of a golden one, does not seem a matter of high moment, nor one fraught with incalculable consequence. And yet on this lesser choice depended all the home-life of the years to come, and the satisfaction or starving of the heart.

There is no need to insist on the alterative power of greater choices. The choice of a wife, of a career, of a friend, is big with blessed or with tragic consequence. But he who is eager to live wisely and to come " smiling from the world's snare uncaught," must note the difference which lesser choices may make.

The choice of one road instead of another; the choice we make of a spot for a short holiday; the choice we make of the books we shall take with us; the choice of the railway-carriage we shall enter, such selections, as every reader of biography knows, may have profound and lasting effects on coming days.

Again Shakespeare reveals to us, half-playfully, how largely choice depends on character. We choose by what we are.

Just as we see, not by the eye but by all that we make ourselves; by every spiritual battle we have won; by every secret sin which we have

cherished ; so in our choices do we betray ourselves, and the habitual tenor of our minds, and
the real values which life has had for us.

The Princes of Morocco and of Aragon are
not just unlucky in their choices. For each of
them the act of a single moment illuminates the
story of a life ; the one coming from a life of
state where " barbaric gold " was the touchstone
of regality ; the other coming with an unhumbled
heart, insolent in the pride of its deservings.

Bassanio came from Venice, and from the
friendship of Antonio. In that splendid friendship he had learned how a man " must give and
hazard all he hath." That most noble of Venetian
merchants, by his venturings on every sea, had
taught him, not by words, the daring that is
needed for success.

One remembers, too, how life had taught
Bassanio how the show of things may be fallacious.
A " swelling port " had been his style of living ;
and the spectacular had brought him to the
miseries of debt. So was Bassanio trained by
friendship and experience to interpret aright the
motto on his casket, and to discount, for the highest
satisfactions, the outward show of gold and silver.

ON THE POWER OF CHOICE

Bassanio chose not by the eye, but by all that
life had brought him ; by his friendships, by his
failures, by his bitter experience of disillusioning ;
and in some such ways do we all make our choices.
We seem to choose quite freely, and yet in every
choice we make, there is the powerful momentum
of our past.

That does not free us from responsibility, as
if choice was necessitated by the strongest motive.
Motives are not like laws of nature, that work
in independence of our will. Our motives are of
our own secret fashioning ; and if we are responsible for them, we are responsible for the choices
which they generate.

Our choices are not fated. Our choices are
the fruits of character. There is a selective power
in character, and for character we are accountable.
We choose, just as we see, by the gathered contents
of our lives ; by our hidden yearnings, our
secret aspirations, our struggles, our sorrows, our
defeats.

When Lot chose the Land of Sodom, he revealed
in a flash his scale of values. When Paul chose to
appeal to Cæsar, he revealed the imperialism of
his heart. When Bassanio chose the leaden casket
he revealed the influence of his friend, and his

hard-won and harsh experience of the deceptiveness of outward show.

Again, half-playfully, Shakespeare suggests to us the inner value of the unattractive. More than once it is the dulness of the lead to which the mind of the reader is directed.

Gold has always an attractive power, and wrought silver is something very beautiful ; but lead is cold and lustreless and dull. It does not charm the senses. We do not fashion ornaments of lead ; but, as the play hints, we use it to enclose the body that lies within the coffin.

It is a fine touch that in the leaden casket lies the portrait of Portia. In that which suggests death are found the lineaments of love and life. And may I not say that he who has not learned the inner value of the unattractive has made little progress in the mastery of life, or in the understanding of the Lord.

Cross-bearing is unattractive, yet it brings the companionship of Christ. Suffering is unattractive, yet what gracious and beautiful things may it conceal. Death is unattractive, yet through death we may be " ever with the Lord," which is "far better" than even married life with Portia.

ON THE POWER OF CHOICE

One great discovery of Jesus was the inner value of the unattractive. In dull and lustreless and heavy people, He found something more beautiful than Portia's likeness. He found the likeness of the Heavenly Father, and a value infinite to Him ; something so precious that it was worth while living for it, and worth while dying for it on the Cross.

Lastly, Shakespeare suggests to us that to win the best we may have to hazard everything. Antonio did that, and Bassanio had to do it, and there come times when everyone must do it.

Lord Kelvin used to say to us that in all his great discoveries there came a point when he had to make a leap into the dark. I believe that, generally, in the spiritual life such a point emerges. We are like drowning men, clinging to a spar— and if we are to be saved, we must let go.

Faith, said Newman, is having the heart to make a venture. Faith is not acceptance of a creed ; it is launching out into the deep. We cling to life and are afraid to hazard it, and then the Lord comes and says to us, " he that loses his life for my sake shall find it."

CHRIST IN SHAKESPEARE

The man of the one talent would not take the hazard, and all the lights of heaven went out for him. The other men of the parable risked everything, and for them the trumpets sounded on the other side. Paul counted all things but dross that he might win Christ and be found in Him. And to win Christ is incomparably finer than Bassanio found it to win Portia.

VIII

ON THE PASSION OF JEALOUSY

(Othello)

THERE is perhaps no play in literature that so grips and moves the heart as does Othello. I can never read it with dry eyes, and I must have read it a score of times.

The ruin of a large and noble nature through the humiliating passion of an insensate jealousy; the helpless suffering of a woman, tortured causelessly like some dumb animal; the diabolical cleverness and coldness of the villain; the infinite pathos of misunderstanding, all these grip the heart with an extraordinary power.

Othello is what I should call a self-contained play. In the other tragedies there is a sense of the unseen, which lifts the action into a certain grandeur, and mitigates the poignancy of feeling. In Othello the vision is contracted, and the emotion correspondingly intensified, to a degree which sometimes is unbearable.

It is generally agreed that Othello was the first tragedy to be written after Hamlet. And while the two plays differ radically, the one a tragedy of thought, the other a tragedy of passion ; there is one feature in which both are alike. Both deal with the effects upon the soul of sudden and overwhelming shock.

With Hamlet it is the overwhelming shock of the discovery of what his mother was. With Othello it is the overwhelming shock of the discovery of what his wife was. One whom each had believed in, and had loved, and on whose pure integrity each would have staked his life, is suddenly revealed as worthless. It makes no difference that, in Othello's case, we recognise the discovery as spurious. To Othello it was just as real as the ghastly exposure of his mother was to Hamlet.

In both plays the shock brings chaos into the ordered world in which the sufferer moves. Hamlet is intellectually paralysed ; Othello is emotionally blinded. The terrific shock which shatters Hamlet's world renders him incapable of action. The terrific shock which wrecks Othello's world turns his love into the fiercest jealousy.

Oftener perhaps than we imagine our whole

world hangs upon one person. Our faith in God, and in humanity, roots in some one person whom we trust. I have known people to lose their faith in heaven, to cease praying, to grow cynical, when someone they believed in proved a sham.

In passing, perhaps I ought to mention that there are critics who dispute this reading of the play. They will not have it that it was jealousy which was the passion of Othello. His revenge was a kind of wild justice ; by killing Desdemona he saved her from herself.

It seems to me that all such criticism rests on a confusion. It confuses the jealousy of little minds with the jealousy of large and generous natures. It expects to find the jealousy of Othello bearing the features of that passion, when it besets little and ignoble souls. Professedly the play deals with jealousy. That is stated over and over again.* Whatever the critics call it, Shakespeare calls it jealousy. And if it shows itself in other ways than those we see in lesser souls, that but reveals (as Shakespeare meant it should) the simple and large greatness of Othello.

* II, i, 310 ; III, iii, 165 *et seq.* ; III, iii, 322-324 ; III, iv, 99 ; III, iv, 157 *et seq.* ; IV, i, 102.

The dominating passion in Othello, then, is jealousy, and the first thing we have to do is to distinguish jealousy from envy.

Now suppose your neighbour has a beautiful garden; you are not jealous of that garden. It is his garden and not yours, and you never talk of being jealous. But you may be envious of that garden, and covet it, and wish that it were yours, and deep down in your heart you may hate the man.

Suppose a man has a splendid library, I should never dream of saying I was jealous of it. It is his library and not mine; he owns it, and not I. I am jealous over my own library, and will not let anybody spoil its books, but I may be envious of his. This means that envy has to do with what belongs to other people; jealousy has to do with something of our own. Envy is the secret coveting of what other people have; jealousy is the passionate possession of one's own. Had Desdemona been anybody else's wife, Othello might have been very envious of her; but Desdemona was his own wife, and he was jealous of her.

It follows that while envy is always a base, mean, grudging thing, jealousy is not inherently a mean thing. Jealousy may be a great and noble passion. Jealousy is the other side of love. It is the guarding of our own. It is the flaming sword of the cherubim at the gate of Paradise. What makes it evil is our sin, just as our sin makes anger evil, so that we hesitate to attribute anger to our Lord.

Sin infects everything; tarnishes everything; leaves its filthy trail on everything; and that is what we mean by total depravity. When we talk of total depravity we do not mean that a man is wholly bad. There are fine things and gleams of heaven in the most degraded of mankind. When we say that a man is totally depraved, we mean that sin has wrought its way into his totality of being. It touches everything within him; it affects every power and faculty; his will, his thought, his imagination, his social outlook, and his passions. Jealousy is the other side of love; it is something intrinsically noble—and then sin enters it and ruins it.

We thus see what the Bible means when it talks of the jealousy of God. "The Lord thy God is a jealous God." Many people do not like the epithet, it has such dark and turbid associations.

But, if what I have been trying to say is true, God without jealousy were not good news. The Greeks thought that the gods were envious, and that, if one were too prosperous, heaven would smite him. There is not a hint in the Bible of such envy; in the Old Testament, prosperity, like that of Solomon, is God's gift. God is jealous of His own. His jealousy is love in action. It is His mighty and magnificent refusal to let any other gods share in His own people. Therefore it is the emotional basis of monotheism. Now think what we owe to monotheism; the unity of character; the progress of the race; the hope of worldwide brotherhood; all scientific progress. So we see that the jealousy of God, His stern intolerance of any rival, is in the highest interests of mankind. God is jealous of His own name, and He is jealous of His children's loyalty, not through any selfish greed to keep all to Himself; but because He knows that on such loyalty depends the moral life of man, and all his growing insight into nature.

It is notable that Shakespeare portrays jealousy in the last man in whom we should look for it.*

* I, iii, 405, 406; II, i, 298; II, iii, 138, III. iv, 26 t seq.

ON THE PASSION OF JEALOUSY

There are men who are naturally jealous; I have heard a wife say (and she was not thinking of this play), "My husband has a terribly jealous temperament, and if he knew, he would kill me." But Desdemona would never have dreamed of saying that of Othello. It was not natural to Othello to be jealous.

So large and generous was his nature, so trustful and confiding, so ready to believe the best of everybody, so free from introspection, that there seemed no room for jealousy in that great heart.

Men who are jealous are generally conscious of inferiority. They feel themselves incompetent to control and keep the devotion of their wives, especially when brilliant and charming and careless Cassios are in the field. No such sense of inferiority ever visited Othello's breast.* Yet it is this man, with his large heart, with his simple and believing soul, whom Shakespeare chooses to display the hateful work of jealousy.

Note how often men are ruined by the last sin you might think they could be guilty of.

* Nor from mine own weak merits will I draw
The smallest fear or doubt of her revolt;
For she had eyes, and chose me.
(III, iii, 187-189.)

8

Moses, meekest of men, sins through an act of hasty and hot anger. Job, whose patience is a proverb, sins through impatience. Othello, with his big nature, that seems to have no room for jealousy, is the victim of that very passion. When anyone is tempted to say, " I could do many bad things, but I never could do *that*," let him be on special guard against *that*, lest just there he be tempted.

But once jealousy is kindled through the malignancy of Iago, note how many things conspire to fan the flame. Did not Desdemona deceive her father whom she loved most tenderly?* Was it impossible then that she should deceive her husband ? And what did Othello know about the life of Venice, or of the way in which the daughters looked at life,† or of how sexual offences were regarded in that metropolis of wealth ? And was he not newly married, and still in the first ecstasies of love, with none of that deep knowledge of his wife which is only gained in the common life of years ? Wooed, too, as she had been, by many gallant and fitting suitors, what

* I, ii, 66 ; I, iii, 294 ; III, iii, 206.

† III, iii, 201 *et seq.*

kind of heart had the woman who could refuse them all and choose a black man ?* For it is difficult for me to doubt, reading the play, that Shakespeare thought of the Moor as black.†

Everything seemed to conspire, once jealousy was born, to aid its rapid growth. Everything fanned the flame. Everything seemed to converge to make that likely which would have been scouted as absurd before. One feels how profoundly true that is of life.

There is a spiritual as well as a material gravitation. Immerse yourself in any study, and you find references to it in every newspaper you open. Let some one dear to you fall ill, with some trouble of which you never heard before, and cases of it spring to your notice every day. Think health, and all the healthful elements of things reveal themselves to you. Make some great decision, and unexpected arguments and reasons fly to you to confirm it.

So was it with Othello. Once jealousy became the ruling passion of his heart, motives and

---

* III, iii, 228 *et seq.*

† E.g., I, i, 88, black ram ; I, ii, 70, sooty bosom ; I, iii, 98, what she fear'd to look on ; I, iii, 291, black ; II, iii, 32, black ; III, iii, 263, black ; III, iii, 387-388, black as mine own face (this alone would be decisive). On the other hand I do not forget that " tawny " Cleopatra says (I, v, 27) " Think on me that am with Phœbus' amorous pinches black."

likelihoods, like unclean birds, came flocking to him. "Where the carcase is, there shall the vultures be gathered together."

It has often been noted how quick Shakespeare is to make great issues hang upon some trifling accident. "Schiller," says Coleridge, "has the material sublime.* To produce an effect he sets you a whole town on fire. Shakespeare drops a handkerchief, and the same or greater effects follow."

Probably there was some incident in his own life which had engraven this truth upon his heart.

> Alas, how easily things go wrong,
> A sigh too deep, or a kiss too long,
> And then a mist or a weeping rain,
> And life is never the same again."

A casual meeting, something trifling and accidental—how often are all the issues of a life bound up with that, and the happiness and tragedy of future years ?

This does not mean, nor did Shakespeare imply, that therefore we are the sport of chance, or the playthings of blind fate. I think Shakespeare would have subscribed to the thought of Wordsworth that God is

> A being whose purposes embrace,
> All accidents.

* Lect. on Shakespeare, *Appendix* (1902), 530.

ON THE PASSION OF JEALOUSY

It was quite a trifling accident that Naboth's vineyard lay contiguous to the gardens of King Ahab. Yet on that hung the ruin of the royal house, and the feasting of the dogs on Jezebel (I Kings xxi).

There is no sin that so distorts the nature as does jealousy; none that so certainly lets loose the hell that is in us all.

> The mind is its own place, and of itself
> Can make a heaven of hell, a hell of heaven.

Ambition may exalt a man. Covetousness may sharpen his wits. Sinful jealousy degrades him always; calls out what is worst in him; destroys his judgment; makes him coarse and cruel, and like another sin, " hardens a' within, and petrifies the feeling." And how unerrringly does Shakespeare portray that in Othello.

He, magnificent in self-control, loses that self-control. He, of dignity unsurpassed in the Shakespearean roll-call, flings his dignity to the winds of heaven. He, true poet and romantic lover, grows coarse, hurls insufferable taunts at " gentle " Desdemona, calls her filthy names, strikes her, and in the end murders her.*

* IV, i, 251 ; IV, ii, 81, 88, 115-121.

Now what are we to make of the moral order of the world where such things happen ? There is no happy ending here—no poetic justice—no interference of high heaven to stop these awful happenings. There is no hint, within the limits of the play, that in a future world there is going to be a recompense for wrong. We are left with the wreckage of happiness ; the ruin of beautiful and noble lives ; the triumph of malignity ; the victory of evil.

Is there then no moral order in the world of Shakespeare ? In his fidelity to fact, and his refusal to say smooth things, are we left in a universe where God is of no account—where there is not justice on the throne—where evil can triumph unimpeded ? Let the answer to that be given by the reader.

Where do his sympathies lie ? Does he crown Iago as a victor ? Does he not deeply feel that Iago (apart from any torture that may await him V, ii, 369) is ruined, lost, and damned, an outcast from the light, unclean, a living death ? And with equal intensity does he not feel, even to the point of tears, that it were ten thousand times better to be Desdemona in her gentleness, ten thousand times better to be Othello, for all his sin and suicide, than the vile wretch whose evil slew them ?

That is the moral power of Shakespeare. He never twists the facts. But he leaves you, in the midst of hideous facts, loathing the evil, cleaving with all your being to what is high and true and good, spite of its sin and failure, and so aligning yourself, perhaps unconsciously, with the Eternal, who reigns, though clouds and darkness are around His throne.

IX

ON THE TRAGEDY OF EGOISM

(Iago)

It is generally agreed that Iago is the most masterly presentation of incarnate evil in the whole of Shakespeare, if not in all literature.

I propose to make a study of his character, based on an independent investigation of the play, and the following are the three points to be considered.

1. What was the character Iago bore in the eyes of men ?

2. What was his real character ?

3. What were his motives in ruining Othello ?

First, then, what was the character Iago bore in the eyes of men ? The chief thing to be noted is that his villainy was entirely unsuspected. Sometimes when the play is acted, there is no mistaking the villain from the moment Iago takes the stage. Wickedness is written large upon him, in his gait, his accent, and his looks ; but that is entirely to misinterpret Shakespeare.

He is called " honest " some seventeen times. Shakespeare is at pains to make it clear that nobody suspected him. If there was one thing that seemed more certain than another it was that he was no hypocrite. He inspired everyone who had dealings with him with a strong confidence in his honesty.

A woman often detects the truth of character better than a man. She has a surer insight. But Desdemona (III, iii, 5) shares with Othello and Cassio (II, iii, 341) the belief in Iago's honesty.

This confidence is greatly strengthened by the apparent downrightness of Iago. He is blunt of speech, pointed and satirical, and careless of offending.

When a man is uniformly gracious, he lays himself open to the charge of insincerity. People are ready to think no man is genuine who is not somewhat brusque and rough in speech. And Shakespeare is at pains to show us that Iago could never be charged with insincerity, by reason of a uniformly gracious tongue. He was never afraid to shock people. He spoke home, as Cassio says (II, i, 166).

We have all known people of kind and tender hearts who were outwardly satirical or cynical. They have adopted a kind of fleering, quizzing manner as a mask to hide the deeps within them. The impression which Iago gave was that he was a man of that kind, whose mockeries were the safeguard of his soul.

Everybody thought him honest. Cassio had never met anyone more kind (III, i, 43). Othello was convinced that he was just (III, iii, 122; V, i, 31). He could be hearty and jovial on occasion (II, iii, 71 *et seq.*). Yet Iago was a consummate villain.

Two questions at once suggest themselves here, and the first is, is this possible? Can anybody go on deceiving everybody as completely as Iago did?

It seems to me we must remember here that Iago was a young man. He was only twenty-eight years old (I, iii, 313). Lincoln said that you can deceive all the people some of the time, and some of the people all the time; but you can't deceive all the people all the time. Iago did not

deceive all the people all the time, for twenty-
eight years is not the span of life. He only
deceived all the people some of the time. Had he
lived on, and never met Othello, sooner or later
he would have been unmasked. The years would
have stripped him bare as winter strips the trees.
But at twenty-eight he was still young, and there
seems to me nothing incredible in the complete-
ness of his deception up till then.

The other question is, Could Iago possibly have
kept it up ? Was he not certain some time to
betray himself, and lift the curtain on his real
being ? I venture to say that Shakespeare
thought of that, and provided as it were a safety-
valve in the intimacy of Iago with Roderigo.

To Roderigo Iago reveals more of his heart than
he does to anybody else. He speaks to Roderigo
with an amazing frankness about the motives
that controlled his actions. And why he should
do so to a blockhead is difficult to understand,
unless Shakespeare had felt the urgent need of
providing some outgate for Iago.

Hypocrisy is an almost intolerable burden.
It overweights the heart. Half-unconsciously
Iago was feeling the enormous burden of duplicity.

It relieved him—it eased the strain—to have one with whom he could be frank, and that one we have in Roderigo.

In attempting, secondly, to get at Iago's real character, we must not forget what a great scholar has pointed out—that Iago is such an accomplished liar that one cannot trust a single word he says about himself.

That he was such a liar is of course evident, and that not only in his great intrigue, for he asserts that Cassio was an habitual drunkard (II, iii, 134), which is not at all necessary to his purpose.

But there are two series of assertions, as it seems to me, in which Iago, speaking of himself, may be regarded as fairly trustworthy.

The one is when he is speaking to Roderigo (v. *ante*), the other, when he is speaking in soliloquy.

Soliloquies in Shakespeare reveal reality. They are the dramatic equivalent of secret thoughts. They are information for the audience of what is locked in the darkness of the heart. And it is notable that in this play brief soliloquies are unusually frequent. I therefore hold that even from Iago's own lips, liar though he was, a certain amount of credible information is to be gained of his true character.

And first, negatively, one must recognise that Iago was no cowardly weakling. He was a man of high, unfailing courage.

Lodovico calls him a very valiant fellow (V, i, 53), implying that such he had proved himself to be, and was so held in general estimation. But it needs no word of Lodovico to certify us of Iago's courage.

In the conduct of his malign intrigue, in his personal bearing in precarious moments ; in his coolness when things were big with peril for him and there was but a step between him and death, Iago displays a superb courage. He never flinches and he never fails. He never loses nerve. If courage is to be equal to one's problem (Emerson), Iago's courage is unimpeachable, and this in the circumstances is notable.

Cunning and hypocrisy are usually associated with a poor spirit. Slippery and subtle knaves, in literature as in life, are commonly poltroons. Iago is of a rarer type. He is diabolically crafty, yet his personal courage is unquestioned.

Again, as we should expect at twenty-eight Iago is not without prickings of his conscience. He is far sunk in evil, but he is not yet spiritually dead. " And what's he then that says I play the villain ? " is one of his utterances in soliloquy (II, iii, 342). Now the truth is that at that stage no one suspected that he was a villain. Iago hears condemning voices, and, though he shrinks from the admission, the voices are those of his own heart.

At this point in the play at any rate, his better nature is not slain. He has not yet quenched the divine spark within him, though he is in imminent peril of so doing. One might say God is still striving with him—and we should never have known it but for this soliloquy, where he betrays that Someone (certainly no intimate) has called him villain.

How often have I seen that in my pastorate ! Men seem hardened, dead in sin, their consciences seared with a hot iron. Yet some moment comes when one has a fleeting glimpse that conscience is not dead.

It seems to me that the truth about Iago is that he is a cold and bloodless egoist. He speaks to Roderigo of a certain kind of men who " keep yet their hearts attending on themselves " (I, i, 51), and he adds, " These fellows have some soul, and such a one do I profess myself." This egoism, cold, calculating, and unscrupulous, controlled by a strong will and powerful intellect, I regard as the secret of Iago.

His hypocrisy is his philosophy. His lying is his plan of action. His falsehood and deceits are not the resorts of cowardice ; they are deliberate moves in the game that he is playing. The service that he gives to others is only an outward show and semblance (I, i, 49 *et seq.*). His real service is always to himself.

When passion would interfere with that, he has a will that crushes passion underfoot (I, iii, 322 *et seq.*). He is his own chief end ; every one else is but a means to that. Self-centred ; self-controlled ; icy and unscrupulous, such is the man who, in an evil hour for both, finds himself confronted with Othello.

Two remarks I should like to add, and the first is this. When anybody is absorbed in self, he almost invariably grows suspicious, and there are many traces in the play that Iago was haunted by suspicion. He was suspicious of Othello (II, i, 394). He was suspicious of Cassio. He suspected beastly things in Desdemona's innocencies (II, i, 262 *et seq.*). To suggest that these suspicions were assumed is utterly to misread the man. Emilia, Iago's wife, knew that he suspected her (IV, ii, 127), even when she was ignorant of his villainy ; and Iago says in a soliloquy (when he is speaking truth)

> the thought whereof
> Doth, like a poisonous mineral, gnaw my inwards.
> (II, i, 305, 6.)

The second is this : When anybody is hideously selfish his world always tends to become hideous. A mean soul lives in a mean world. " We aye get what we bring," said Duncan Matheson.

There is a strange selective power in personality. " Tell me what you see," said one, " and I shall tell you what you are." And we can tell what Iago is by the reflection of his soul on the moral world in which he found himself.

For him there was nothing noble there ; nothing beautiful or pure. Reputation was an imposition (II, iii, 269). Love was but lust (I, iii, 336). It was an impoverished and debased world, and everything fine or fair in it a fraud, because his own life was a fraud, and his soul debased and impoverished through selfishness.

Lastly we consider what were Iago's motives in ruining Othello. To begin with we must discuss the view first suggested by Coleridge, that Iago's malignancy was motiveless. That is to say, no motives were required. Iago acted so through sheer delight in evil. He had said, " Evil, be thou my good." He had sold himself to Satan. It was as natural for him to pursue villainy as for certain flowers to open in the night, and any alleged motives are but pretexts—" the motive-hunting of motiveless malignity."

Now it is a question whether any man ever possesses such a nature. Mephistopheles in Goethe does, but then Mephistopheles is not a man. But apart from that it seems to me that Shakespeare clearly indicates a motive, and means it to be accepted as the real one.

That motive is hatred of Othello, and the reality of that hatred is hinted at in this, that Shakespeare brings it forward in the very opening of the play (I, i, 7, 8).

Four times in the first Act Iago dwells on his

hatred of Othello, and each time in talk with Roderigo, with whom he allows himself unusual frankness. " I do hate him as I do hell pains " (I, i, 155) does not suggest deception ; and it is because of this hatred that his " cause is hearted " (I, iii, 373), that is, lodged within his heart.

Scholars seek to discredit this, by stating that we only hear of this hatred in the first Act. That is not the case (II, i, 297). But even if it were, it seems to me to tell the other way. At the very opening of the play Shakespeare is revealing to his audience the powerful motive in Iago's heart for the villainy that is to follow.

And that there were reasons for this hatred in Iago's breast becomes patent as we read. First there was the rankling grudge that Othello had not made him his lieutenant (I, i). Second, there was the deep suspicion that Othello had betrayed his wife Emilia (v. *ante*). Anybody who knows human nature will recognise that these two causes, blending, are ample to stir up in any heart a hatred as of hell.

Because there are two reasons for his hate, Coleridge holds that Iago is " motive hunting." He might as well charge Shylock with motive hunting because he also has two reasons for his hate.

> I hate him for he is a Christian ;
> But more for that in low simplicity
> He lends out money gratis.

If anything is clear to me, it is that the two causes to Iago are intensely real, and that the so caused hatred inspired the hideous villainy, which forms the story of the play.

X

ON THE SOVEREIGNTY OF LOVE

(ROMEO AND JULIET)

ROMEO AND JULIET has the distinction of being the first tragedy of Shakespeare. There is the evidence of different versions which survive that he worked at it long and carefully. It is a matter of deep interest that we still have the original on which Shakespeare based his play, a poem by Arthur Brooke. And to read that poem, and compare it and contrast it with the drama, throws light on the genius of Shakespeare.

Now the great message of this glorious drama is the sovereignty of love. But before we discuss that, there are one or two cognate matters to be touched upon.

One thing, for instance, that strikes everybody,

on a first reading of the play, is the fact that
Romeo, until the moment that Juliet appears,
is deeply in love with another woman, Rosaline.
Now this is not original with Shakespeare. It is
found in Brooke's poem. And the question at
once arises, why did Shakespeare retain it ? Would
it not have added to the attractiveness of Romeo,
to the worth of his love for Juliet, if Shakespeare
had ignored this, and made love for Juliet the
first and only passion of Romeo's heart ? When
Goethe put Romeo and Juliet on the stage at
Weimar, he omitted Rosaline.

Probably the reason for its retention is this.
Just as there are some men, like Hamlet, who
cannot live save in the exercise of reflection, so
there are others for whom life is barren save in
the enjoyment and exercise of love. They are
in love with love. They live and move and have
their being not in the cold activities of intellect,
but in the glowing emotions of the heart, and such
an one was Romeo.

Without love he could not live. Unless he
" walked in love," life was " flat, stale, unprofit-
able " to him. The fact that Romeo from the
first moment that we hear of him is under love's

dominion, illuminates, as nothing else could do, the kind of man he was.

That is why Shakespeare retains Rosaline. Romeo was not a man surprised by love ; not one (like Antony) wrested from other aims and interests by the grip of sudden passion ; he was a man who always dwelt in his emotions, and for whom love was life.

Again I think it would be true to say (and it is a very important thing to say) that for Shakespeare all love was in its essence one.

The Greeks had different names for different kinds of love ; but it is a question if Shakespeare (who knew little Latin and less Greek) would have tolerated any such sharp cleavages.

Nothing could be more lofty or spiritual than the love of Juliet. The dullest must feel that it is dazzlingly pure. Yet in that love are all the elements of sense, and a frank and joyous acknowledgment of the mystery of sex.

With Shakespeare there are not different kinds of love, but different proportions in the various elements of which all love is compounded. The love which is heavenly and holy is not the love which despises or ignores the sensuous, as though it had its being in a different world ; but that which subdues and irradiates the sensuous in the sovereignty of what is spiritual.

In such books as the Song of Solomon (for all who read it mystically), and the Letters of Samuel Rutherford, and many of the sermons of McCheyne, there is that fearless and frank acceptance of the facts of life, inherent in and transmuted by the highest, which, in the sphere of drama, is the characteristic attitude of Shakespeare.

Again it has been noted that love rarely grows in Shakespeare. It leaps full-grown into life, and is reciprocal.

One thinks of Rosalind and Orlando ; of Ferdinand and Miranda ; and here of Romeo and Juliet. There is even the suggestion of a higher power at work, drawing lives together irresistibly, as by some heavenly gravitation.

Now this is not the invariable way of love, for there are many to whom it has gradually come. This, of course, Shakespeare knew, e.g. Desdemona and Othello. There are many who could not give the day or hour when love began to blossom in the breast. But the very fact that Shakespeare, with his matchless insight into life, should lay such stress on great transforming moments surely ought to make us very chary of decrying their occurrence in the soul.

Sudden conversions of the soul are no more unusual than the sudden love of Shakespeare. They may be as lasting in their consequences as the swift-born love of Romeo and Juliet. Nobody saw more clearly than Shakespeare did that a moment may alter everything, and change character to its very depths.

Nowhere, again, more clearly than in this play do we see how skilfully Shakespeare uses nature to throw up in relief the passions of the heart.

There are two contrasted ways of viewing nature in reference to human passions. One emphasises the unconcern of nature to the joys and sorrows of humanity. The birds sing on though human hearts are breaking. The flowers are beautiful though life is grey. This unconcern, this want of sympathy, has often wrung the heart of poets, as it wrung the heart of Robert Burns.

The other finds in nature a mystical corre-spondence with the passions. It discovers the moods of men reflected in the aspects of the world. It therefore feels at liberty, in literature, to heighten the impression of emotion by making nature intensely sympathetic.

When our Lord was crucified there was darkness from the sixth hour till the ninth. Nature was sympathising with that dark deed of shame and cruelty. Shakespeare, with consummate art, carries over into the realm of poetry what in history was exemplified at Calvary.

One recalls the storm on the heath in King Lear ; the fair and foul day when the witches hail Macbeth ; the night of glamour when Lorenzo and Jessica make love ; the night of tempest and of prodigy before the fall of Julius Cæsar. So here the throbbing background, the heat and languor and passion of Italian nights at midsummer, accords with, and throws into relief, the human tragedy of love and sorrow.

Most of us would say that this is only the pathetic fallacy. We interpret nature by our own experiences, and read there what we want. Shakespeare as dramatist goes farther, and recognises a pre-established harmony between the joys and sorrows of his heroes, and the nature which is the background of them all.

To come then to the lessons of the drama, inwrought into the fabric, I should put first the truth that nobody can isolate experience. What I mean by that is this.

Love is the most absorbing of all passions. The lover has no thought but for the loved one. Lover and beloved seem to stand apart, separated from the world. And one great lesson of the play is this (and everybody has to learn it) that you cannot isolate love, or uproot it from social environment.

The play does not open with Romeo and Juliet. It opens with the enmity of Capulet and Montague. From that, do what they will, Romeo and Juliet never can get clear. They may be all the world to one another, but the environing world is real nevertheless, and in ways the lovers never reckoned on, it insists on being recognised.

A young fellow may say, " I'm going to marry her ; I'm not going to marry her family or relations." He imagines he can isolate his love. But life will teach him, just what Shakespeare teaches, and what the Bible taught us long ago, that no man liveth to himself.

Every passion has its social bearings. Passion cannot be wrested from environment. We love

138

not in a vacuum, but in a world of Capulets and
Montagues. The play that is going to portray
to us an absorbing and commanding passion,
begins with the servants of the embittered houses
biting their thumbs at one another.

But if Shakespeare in his fidelity insists on that,
there is something else he equally insists on. It
is that love is stronger than everything that
separates.

We see the houses of Capulet and Montague.
They are old and embittered enemies. Their
feud is the cause of constant quarrelling. It
descends even to the servants. Yet when love
is born, everything goes down ; every barrier is
broken ; every wall of partition is removed.

What experience could not do ; what the
counsels of old age could not accomplish ; what
the command of authority was powerless to
achieve, love did, and did triumphantly. And
then one thinks of Somebody who died for us and
lives, and who in a world of bitter separations,
says, " Children, have you tried the way of
love ? "

In Verona it was not an idle dream—the
power of love to break through all that separates.

Men saw the old antagonisms swept aside there by the mighty tide of love. One wonders why it should be an idle dream, in a world which is but Verona writ large, and which teems with Capulets and Montagues.

Everything else has been tried and has failed; all has been lacking in a uniting power. Men thought that commerce and common interests would unite men—and then the Great War came. Why not listen to the voice of Him (whom the old friar in Verona loved), who is still among us, and still saying softly, " Children, have you tried the way of love ? "

Again we are taught this lesson in the play, that a deep, real love liberates character.

When he loves Rosaline, Romeo is not himself, as his friends are swift to notice. He is affected, pedantic, melancholy. He affects solitude and shuns company. He hides himself even from the eye of day. But from the hour that his whole being is possessed by love for Juliet, there moves on a liberating process, through which there emerges the true Romeo.

His intellect awakes, to the amazement of Mercutio, whom he can match now in a play of wits. His imagination deepens and expands. His will becomes steadily more strong—all under the releasing power of love.

And so it is with Juliet. When we first meet her she is a child, not yet fourteen years of age, thinking and speaking as a child, and rendering the obedience of a child. Then a great love grips her, and it ripens her, and she becomes a woman. Now she can defy her father and her mother. She can scorn the tradition of her house. She can rise above the atmosphere of hate in which she had been reared. And all this enrichment in intellect and will and character for her too, as for Romeo, is wrought by love.

It was Henry Drummond who called love the greatest thing in the world. With that Shakespeare would agree. In the power to liberate character, to reveal all that is best, to develop every faculty until a man can be himself, there is nothing that can equal love.

Lastly, Shakespeare would have us learn that love is the great reconciler. For the play closes, not with death alone, but with the reconciliation of the divided houses. The feud is laid aside ; the old enmity is buried ; the estrangement ends ;

the alienation is removed, and all this through a love that was so deep and true that it brought the hearts which cherished it to death.

Love was the mediator, love that did not count the cost ; love that for the joy that was set before it went down into the darkness of the grave. And though Shakespeare does not point us to the road that leads to the place called Calvary, do we not catch a glimpse of that way of sorrows ; and hear on it, far off, the footfall of One who loved unto the uttermost, and loving died, and dying achieved a mightier reconciliation than any that Verona ever knew ?

Printed in the United States
123075LV00002B/51/A